CITY OF ASPINWALL.

PANAMA IN 1855.

AN ACCOUNT OF

THE PANAMA RAIL-ROAD,

OF THE

CITIES OF PANAMA AND ASPINWALL,

WITH SKETCHES OF

LIFE AND CHARACTER ON THE ISTHMUS.

BY ROBERT TOMES.

NEW YORK:
HARPER & BROTHERS, PUBLISHERS,
FRANKLIN SQUARE.
1855.

PREFACE.

This little book is a record of observations made during a short residence on the Isthmus of Panama, under circumstances very favorable for the acquisition of such information as it is thought the public desire to have.

While the author has striven to make his book useful as a guide to the traveler, and instructive to those interested in the commercial development of the Isthmus, under the auspices of the Panama Railroad, he has endeavored to give a picturesque interest to his work which may render it acceptable to the general reader.

That the lively parts of his book may not be deemed frivolous by one class of readers, and the serious found dull by the other, is the hope of

THE AUTHOR.

New York, *June 9th*, 1855.

CONTENTS

PANAMA IN 1855.

CHAPTER I.

"WOULD YOU LIKE TO GO TO PANAMA?" was the question propounded to me by a friend on one of the bitterest of the cold days of a New York January. While thawing my frozen fingers with the breath which steamed out of my mouth, and fell condensed in a rime of frost upon the beard, I warmed up at once at the proposition, and my imagination, like a migratory bird, fluttered away from its forced hibernation in my "cold, uncomfortable body," shivering in an atmosphere which scorned double-milled pilot cloth with the coolest contempt, and sunk the thermometer into a degree of littleness to which 0 (zero) would have been an unexpected relief, and the freezing-point a hopeless aspiration. My imagination was at once basking in a

Southern sun and all a-glow with a tropical fervor. So when my friend strengthened his proposition with the comforting assurance "that it would cost me nothing," and smacked his eloquent lips over the dainty prospect he described of I don't know how many dozen-dozens of Champagne, rounds of beef, and other generous elements of the feasts in liberal contemplation, I smacked my lips in response, and closed at once. A few days subsequently—the thermometer in the mean time falling as my hopes of escape were rising—I received the following note, which I put on record as a model invitation to be commended as an example to all givers of hospitality:

OFFICE OF THE PANAMA RAILROAD COMPANY,
NEW YORK, *January 25th*, 1855.

DEAR SIR,

The Panama Railroad having been so far completed as to admit of the trains passing from Ocean to Ocean, the Board of Directors desire that the work should be visited by a delegation of Stockholders and others interested in the enterprise, to commemorate this important event.

A limited number of invited guests are expected to go out in the Steamer *George Law*, on the 5th proximo, under the direction of Wm. Whitewright, Jr., Esq., one of the members of the Board, and you are respectfully invited to accompany the party at that time.

You will confer a favor by an early reply, signifying your acceptance of this invitation, or otherwise, so that the Company may have the opportunity to extend this courtesy to some other gentleman, should you be unable to honor the occasion by your presence.

In behalf of the Board of Directors,
Very respectfully,
Your obed't Serv't,
DAVID HOADLEY, Pres't.

Here was a magnificent proffer of hospitality; a corporate host representing I don't know how many hundred thousands of stock and bondholders, with millions of money at its command, stretching out its Briarean hands, with its gigantic grasp of welcome, and taking to its generous embrace a poor devil of an author, whose last work had but provided for his sparse washerwoman's bill, and secured him the small honor of a "tea and turn-out," where he had roared as mildly as any sucking dove for the small consideration of a cup of dilute bohea.

I accepted the invitation, of course; proudly repressing the sense of personal obligation, by adroitly descanting, in my note of acceptance, upon the great occasion, to use the modest railroad phrase, "of the trains passing from ocean to ocean." I would be *pleased*, I said, to bear my humble share in "commemorating the important event." I had written *very happy*, having for a moment given way to the enthusiasm of my feelings, when, after some reflection, I substituted *pleased*, as the term more appropriate to the cool indifference of the independent man of the world, and the importance of a guest solicited to share in the festivities of an august corporation.

An interview with the representative of the Board of Directors followed, and I looked upon this gentleman—the impersonation of the Great Railroad Company, in whom was concentrated the gigantic hospitality of which I had been invited to partake—with a sentiment of sublime respect, not unmingled with a substantial sense of satisfaction, especially as he confirmed, word for word, all my friend's glowing description of the rounds of beef, and the dozens of Champagne in prospect. I was somewhat surprised, on first sight, at the moderate dimensions of this gentleman, as my imagination had swelled him, in his corporate capacity of the impersonated Railroad host, to something tremendous: but when I took a common-sense view of his well-developed person, in which the hardness of youthful muscle was fast softening into the unctuousness of increasing age and obesity, and when I observed that the restless expression of eager youth was now beginning to repose in the comfortable self-satisfaction of middle life, I consoled myself for the disappointment of my imagination, by the reasonable expectations such a good-looking, well-ordered, respectable personage was calculated to inspire.

I learned from him how some seventeen of us, under his hospitable guidance and by the generous invitation of the Panama Railroad Company, were to be conveyed from New York, on the 5th of February, to the Isthmus of Darien, in the steamer *George Law*, *gratuitously;* how we were to be wined and brandied on board, *gratuitously;* how we were to be boarded and lodged and doctored at Aspinwall, *gratuitously;* how we were to be conveyed in triumph over the Railroad, *gratuitously;* how we were to be banqueted at Panama, and might immortalize ourselves in speeches on the occasion, *gratuitously;* how we might stay a fortnight on the Isthmus, to wander among its tropical delights, or to stretch ourselves beneath the shade of its beautiful mangroves, in the agonies of Chagres fever, *gratuitously;* and how, finally, we were to be conveyed home, by the steamer to New York, and wined and brandied as on the trip outward, *gratuitously.*

This was certainly a brilliant programme, and I readily put myself down as a humble performer on the occasion. I am bound to say, as will appear in the course of this veritable history, that the Railroad Company was faithful to its contract, in every respect, with the exception of the very important provision as to brandy and wine. Dick, the negro steward of the Illinois, will testify in any court of law that I paid him two dollars and a half in gold for one bottle of sherry—which Lord C. pronounced execrable, but drank his fair share of it nevertheless, though, as he protested, under excitement—and two dollars, in a bankable bill, for one bottle of brandy, the qualities of which I'll leave to negro Dick, as he has been called into court, to vouch for, since he enjoyed the most frequent, though stealthy, opportunities of forming a judgment.

Collecting together the remnant of my last summer's wardrobe, hurrying through the wash the week's linen, quieting the preposterous anxieties of my tailor with assurances of a short absence, proudly settling his account with a promise to pay on my return, packing my portmanteau and taking a parting cup with some trusty friends, I yielded myself up incontinently to the hospitality of the Panama Railroad Company, on the fifth day of February, eighteen hundred and fifty-five.

As the City Hall clock was fast approaching the hour of two, I hurried down Warren Street, with my eye fixed upon the tall chimney of the steamer *George Law*, which was throwing out its black banner of smoke, and signalizing approaching departure. On arriving at the dock I made my way aboard, under the cover of an iron-bound portmanteau, which staggered high upon the unsteady shoulders of a profane dock lad, whose dirty, ragged appearance, and by no means clean or tidy observations, cleared the road, like a pestilence, through the confused crowd of loaded-down hackney-coaches, mysteriously involved with heaped-up carts, of eager, hurrying passengers, staggering porters, drunken sailors and firemen, bellowing orange-women, shouting boys, and of blubbering women and children, that thronged the dock and the passages to the steamer.

The bell of the steamer clinked an impatient warning; "Clear the gangways for the mails," hoarsely roared a gusty mate; helter-skelter thronged the crowd ashore; tingle, tingle whispered the Captain's bell from the wheel-house, to which the engine responded with a loud snort, and threw out its gigantic arms in preparatory struggle, provoking the waters into a seething agony of rage. "Let go that hawser," cried the pilot, as his hand waved "a-port your helm" to the man at the wheel, and the *George*

Law was in a moment out in the stream, away from the shouts of the multitude which thronged the pier, and I was left to contemplation and my cigar.

With a brisk northwest wind, the tide ebbing out and a full head of steam, the "*Law*," though no witch on the water, spared but little time for sentimental regrets of home. She rapidly cleared the teeming city, and its docks choked full with shipping, passed Governor's Island, with its winter mantle of snow, looking like a bank of ice floating in the bay, and hurried along Staten Island, with its Quarantine of bilious lazar-houses and hospitals, and its contrasting homes of wealth and comfort sending up from their firesides, into the cold air, a cheerful indication of enjoyment, in the smoke which wound through the valleys and wreathed about the snowy summits of the hills. The ship thence steamed through the Narrows into the lower bay, sending a graceful farewell courtesy to the land in her waving wake along the shore of Sandy Hook, and shaking out all her canvas drapery, strode gallantly on to sea.

It was astonishing how soon their appropriate places were found by some four hundred and fifty people, which was about the number of the passengers on the *George Law*, who, with their miscellaneous baggage of countless portmanteaus, square, angular unyielding chests, unaccommodating bandboxes, irresponsible packages, stray parcels, and their own diverse dispositions seemed at the start a mysterious problem of crowded confusion, impossible of solution. While, however, the heights of Neversink were still rising clear in the evening sun, and the steamer had just begun to stagger in her sea gait, at the hour our fashionable friends we had left behind in New York were sitting down to dinner, almost every man, woman, and child of the four hundred and fifty, with their several baggage accompaniments, was snugly stowed away. The sea-change, which was beginning to operate on the landsmen, had something to do, doubtless, with this rapid precipitation below. Cigars had long since ceased to console, brandy-and-water had been drunk and drunk again, and at last given up in hopeless despair, vigorous resolutions not to yield a jot had been rapidly losing their hold, and the sound of *he-e-ve-ur-ur-p*, which soon issued from the state-rooms, showed that the good resolutions were being abandoned, in common with the contents of the stomach.

The deck was left, at an early hour in the evening, clear to a few old salts, among whom my marine experiences entitle me to class myself. The cigars of these waned out, one after the other, and they turned in below to brandy-and-water and to bed, leaving me alone to solitary contemplation of the night upon the ocean, with all the starry host of the heavens looking down upon me, and the great sea roaring, heaving, and flashing its phosphorescent fire on every side of the tossed ship. But my thoughts turned from these sublimities, and wandered back to the humble fireside of home, and the gentle affections and cosey comforts which nestled about it.

I lengthened out my solitary walk that night on the swaying deck of the ship; for the comfortable imaginings of home were far more agreeable than a hurried observation of my cell, which the steamboat proprietors had dignified with the lofty appellation of *state* room, led me to anticipate would be the realities of my nocturnal experiences at sea.

To the untraveled experience of a landsman, there is something startling in the announcement, as he reads his morning paper, of a California steamer carrying some fifteen hundred passengers, the population of a fair sized county-town; but his surprise gives way when he is once booked, ticketed, packed, and shipped in one of those floating herring-boxes. Let him be tall or short, stout or meagre, he must submit to the inexorable fate of 5 × 2, preordained by the absolute will of the steam-boat proprietary for their own wise purposes. The "*George Law*" on this occasion was not crowded, and each *state* room no bigger, on my honor, than my clothes-closet at home, the old coat hanging in which I could not help envying for its comparative stateliness of provision and comfort, contained *only* three passengers. Where the fourth was to be put in the emergency of a crowd, I could not devise with all my newly developed experience of the infinite adaptation of limited space to unlimited numbers.

In No. 40 we were three, and by a ready instinct of self-preservation, it was mutually conceded, without a word of preliminary negotiation, but purely from the force of necessity, that no two should attempt to stand on the floor together. It was, in fact, utterly incompatible with personal individuality. When No. 1 turned in, Nos. 2 and 3 kept out; when No. 3 turned out, Nos. 1 and 2 staid in their beds, if it is permissible to call those three hard boards which were laid across the room, upon which we nightly shelved ourselves, beds, as we are bound to do, perhaps from the fact of their being spread with a very thin slice of mattress and closed in with a dingy gauze curtain. Taking one's place—I speak for No. 2—upon his appropriate shelf was a very mysterious operation, of which the sufferer can only recollect, by the reminder of a broken head and a pair of bruised knees, the pains and penalties—a remembrance strengthened, however, by a very lively recollection of the curses of his fellow miserables, who protested vigorously against the effects of the operation upon themselves; he—No. 1—on the shelf above denying emphatically any one's claim but his own to the hair of his head, and he—No. 2—on the shelf below refusing as positively to being kicked on the occasion. So with grasping the hair of one, and lodging my feet in the body of the other—a process which I must do my fellow-sufferers the justice of acknowledging that they bore with exemplary resignation after a few days of compulsory habit—I managed to get upon the middle shelf, where, from pure fatigue from hard work, and with a flexible temper which happily can bend to any thing, even to a berth in the *George Law*, I managed to sleep and be content.

Night over, the gong roared out its early call, and the morning sun blazed through the port-hole like a great burning-glass, awaking No. 1 to the matutinal duty of a call upon "Steward! steward! I say, steward, a glass, some iced water, and that ——;" with which Nos. 2 and 3, protesting mildly at first, soon learned to conform. When that infernal gong ceased to roar, No. 1, having dismissed the steward, and smacked his lips with the satisfaction of a man who had fulfilled the first duty of the day, tumbled out, went through the absurd practice of shaving his beard and cutting his face, dressed himself, and proceeded to ventilate on deck. No. 2, then poising himself upon the rim of his shelf, and waiting anxiously for a convenient pitch of the ship, also tumbled out, and securing his back against the berth, his abdomen (the polite appellation we believe) against the wash-stand, propping his starboard with the baggage, and his port-side with the door, went through the small ablutions and meagre course of toilet to which the traveler by sea has to resign himself. Thus began the second day of the voyage.

A notice to passengers conspicuously posted about the cabin and the deck to the effect that no deadly weapons were to be worn, no fire-arms discharged, and no person was to appear at table with his coat off, was calculated to awaken in the heart of a timid traveler a fear of his personal security by no means encouraging. A bloody vision of deadly encounter, the brandishing of bowie-knives, the flashing of revolvers, and the other rude exercises of Californian discipline, startled the imagination, and sent it cowering to the security of New York, under the protection of that civic Draco, Mayor Wood. Discipline at sea is an excellent thing, but a little more of the substance, and much less of the show of it, would be an improvement.

Thus, too, most travelers go to sea with a dislike to drowning, and are pleased to find every security against so disagreeable an incident; but they do not care to be constantly reminded of the danger as they are by the display on board the *George Law*, of what the imaginative steamboat proprietors are pleased to call "life-preservers." The traveler shall find conspicuously hung up in each state-room a collection of yellow painted tin cylinders, which, after a day or two, he will puzzle his understanding, with the aid of the experience of the steward, into comprehending to be intended for the protection of his life. If he counts the half dozen boats which hang so lightly in the air on the ship's quarters, calculates the chances of a passage in a scramble for life of a thousand human beings in the despair of a sinking ship, if he looks in vain for the full complement of oars, marks the deficiency of row-locks, discovers the absence of the rudder, casts a knowing eye through the plug-holes down into the abyss of the ocean below, and anxiously searches for the corresponding plugs and don't find them, he will turn with some degree of reverence to those tin cases—the skeletons in his cabin—which hang as ghastly *memento moris* above his head. If he is at all curious—as I do not recommend him to be, provided he values his ease of mind—he will find, if he has had any hope in those tin things, he has been a victim of misplaced confidence, and will see that, although like a millstone about the neck, they might assist in expediting the agony, they can not prevent it. Let him console himself then with the joke, as my friend M—— did, that those who go to sea preserve the flesh of human creatures in tin-cans, as they do that of other beasts!

Thank Heaven, there was no necessity of testing the sinking qualities of the metallic life-preservers, as there seemed to be no need of thundering out anathemas from the main-mast against the murderous propensities of bowie-knives and six-barreled revolvers. The only pistols, I am bound to say, I saw on board was a brace of Colt's, in the safe hands of an American Consul, a fellow-passenger, who also, to the best of my belief, was the sole transgressor of the shirt sleeve ordinance, although there were some suspicions of a similar offense resting upon the character of the United States Minister Plenipotentiary to New Granada.

Four hundred and fifty—two hundred cabin, and the rest steerage—was the number of passengers, most of whom were bound to California. The Californians still clung to their red shirts, the slouched hat, the capacious boots, the girdled trowsers, the flowing blankets, and other loose characteristics of dress, although they had for the most part abandoned the free habits of life which in the first days of the murderous bowie-knife and deadly revolver emigration to the gold region distinguished our adventurous countrymen. There were but few who were going now for the first time to California, although there were still some untried diggers, showing that the first passion for gold was yet burning in the heart of the people. In the steerage the greater part was composed of sturdy-willed and strong-armed laborers, some few of whom were accompanied by their wives and children, who having once earned a fair day's wages for a fair day's work in California, could not be content with what seemed to their enlarged desires the paltry price of labor at home. These, dignified with the self-respect of independence, seemed to yield with no dissatisfaction to their harder lot in the steerage, and kept forward patiently within the inevitable gate, watched by a vigorous sea-Cerberus, which barred them from all communication with the more pretentious cabin passengers. Their spirits did not yield a jot to the hard necessities of two in a bunk, and of salt grub six days out of seven, but merrily overflowed in boisterous talk and in negro songs, as they lounged upon their blue and red blankets spread upon the forward deck. Their quarters were clean, well-ventilated, and, apart from the practice of bringing two strangers at once into the close intimacy of bed-fellows, well ordered. The females were only guarded from intrusion by the scant protection of a canvas curtain, and trusted themselves with confiding faith to the universal gallantry of the men in America, whether of broadcloth or red flannel. The food served up was plain and substantial; and I for one, after the first day's experience of cabin fare, would have been happy to have exchanged our cook's absurd attempts to translate the French cuisine into his own idiomatic Irish, for the native pork and beans upon which the hearty fellows of the steerage were, much to my envy, daily fattening.

The two hundred in the cabin, were chiefly composed of returning Californian bankers, merchants, and tradesmen, whose fictitious successes or genuine means seemed to justify the expense of the apocryphal luxury of a first-class passage. Aged matrons, youthful expectant mothers, and a swarming host of tokens of conjugal affection—children of all ages—secured to the well-wisher of his race the daily prospect of all the domestic relations from fond connubiality to conjugal satiety. There was a runaway couple from the West, who were provokingly tender on every public occasion, and several experienced pairs, who did not await a private opportunity to exhibit their mutual discontent.

Ten days at sea will disclose more of intimate character than a life-time on land. After the first day's familiarity with the novelties of a sea-voyage, men and women, away from the usual distractions of business, pleasure, and ever-recurring incident and event of life on land, are thrown entirely upon their personal resources, which bring out all the characteristic elements of disposition, and whether you love or hate your fellow-creatures the more in consequence of the revelation it is not safe to say.

Macaulay says somewhere, that the only diversion for the male traveler at sea is to quarrel with his own sex, and fall in love with the opposite. There was no very vigorous manifestation during the voyage of masculine pugnacity, but a very intense degree of the development of feminine coquetry, briskly responded to by some of the more susceptible. How the warm tropics expanded the young affections! How they would shrink languishing from the garish sun and ever-present eye of daily observation, and how revive in the shade and seclusion of evening, and in the invigorating breeze of the trade-winds! Those nocturnal promenades on deck beneath the glorious heavens of the tropical summer, showed doubtless an elevated sense of the celestial sublime; but, it is suspected, not unalloyed with a full appreciation of the beauty of things terrestrial. I give Miss —— full credit for the genuineness of her admiration as she exclaimed, "Look, what a pretty star!" when I stupidly intruded one night upon a *tête-à-tête* behind the capstan, between the above Miss —— and a certain —— (I can swear to the whiskers). There seemed, however, no especial reason to continue that astronomical observation, night after night, and prolong it many hours after the peremptory steward had put out the lights in the cabin, and hung up the dim round lantern which cast its winking glimmer like a sleepy eye upon the closed doors of the state-rooms and the boots and shoes of their snoring occupants. It was time for Miss —— and Mr. ——, like all respectable people, to be in bed.

There was one indefatigable coquette, a mettlesome damsel, whose expansive graces and free-and-easy manners had been developed in the wilds of the West. By Jingo (her favorite expression) the wicked wags called her, and there was not a youth aboard who had reached the maturity of whiskers that had not basked in her diffusive charms. Mamma was too much subdued by sea-sickness to exercise any vigor of maternal discipline, and papa only indulged in a faint protest during the intervals of poker and brandy toddy. But By Jingo carried the day, and the night, too; had her own way, and led all the men into it in the bargain. The old salt, Captain S——, in spite of threescore, and the vivid recollection of Mrs. S—— at home, gave in finally, and was caught one day tying a knot in her streaming hair, which operation the old skipper was pleased to term taking in a reef, "as the dashing little craft was making too much headway in such a sea." But By Jingo has long since reached her destination, and it is hoped she may be safely moored at home, and not again trusted at sea without the safe convoy of a marital cruiser.

Each day, with the intimacy so characteristic of the unreservedness of a sea voyage, revealed scores of new acquaintances. There was the United States Minister Plenipotentiary, a slouchy Western politician and judge of decided national predilections, who chewed vigorously and spat enormously, keeping the man busy with his swab who was especially detailed for that service. There was the United States Consul to Panama, whose acquaintance I had the honor of making, a militia Colonel, and veteran torso, who had left a leg in Mexico, and disposed of an arm in a scuffle in Texas. He made up for his loss of limbs, however, by a very vigorous use of their wooden substitutes, and showed his energy of character by falling out with every one, and shaking his false arm and stamping his false leg with immense vigor. One little pale-faced woman was terribly startled when the formidable Colonel, preparatory to a siesta on deck, where he was fond of displaying his huge dismembered body in the scantiest of drapery, shook out one day his frouzy blanket, declaring that it was twenty-five years old, and that it had fallen into his possession as booty after he had killed the owner. The Colonel had a magnificent brace of silver-plated Colt's revolvers, which he was fond of exhibiting, and of which, it is hoped, his bellicose qualities will not lead him to any dangerous usage. He is not as highly valued in Panama as such a representative of our country should be, probably because the rude Border style of the man falls somewhat short, as it must be confessed, of the high standard of Castilian manners.

One day I was received, over a bottle of bitter ale, into the confidence of a brisk Californian trader, who was largely in the book and stationery line, and who disclosed to me how he scattered books and newspapers broadcast over the States of Oregon and California; how he diffused over those benighted lands the civilizing literature of 1000 *Harper's Magazine*, monthly, for the small consideration of twenty cents a number, of 9000 *New York Heralds*, an equal number of *Tribunes*, 13,000

Boston Journals, and 11,000 of the *Courrier des Etats Unis* fortnightly, at the moderate price of ten cents each copy, and how in fact he paid no less than $40,000 annually for newspapers alone. But this was nothing to the wonders revealed of another Californian—a primitive settler who, some twenty years ago, had fled ashore a runaway sailor, and now possessed 300 miles of land, and 12,000 head of cattle, worth at the butchers' stall in San Francisco $30 a head at the lowest computation; and there were others whose boasted possessions and grandiose incomes made an Astor of each of them; but it is hoped all was well-garnered before the universal financial tornado which lately swept California into bankruptcy. Then among the notabilities I renewed my acquaintance with my old friend, the agent R—— of Dana's Defoe-like narrative, whose marriage there so graphically described gives him a reasonable expectation of a fair share of old Norriega's leagues of California land, and unlimited herds of cattle which run wildly upon it. Among the passengers, too, there was the tragic actress who had made "her last appearance with great applause" at the Broadway previous to embarking for the fulfillment of her California engagement, but whose sock and buskin did not at all appear to aid her in the acquisition of those useful but not very dramatic sea-legs, of which the nautical discourse. Her walk was certainly not altogether of the high tragedy style, although sea-sickness gave a very melodramatic twinge to her expressive face. Such were the companions of the voyage in addition to the seventeen railroad guests, and a miscellaneous crowd of Californian traders, all with the unmistakable swagger of the denizens of a "great country," merchants of South America, mercantile travelers to China, Panama railroad officials, Jew peddlers, and uncertain adventurers.

Even a brief ten days' sea-voyage exhausts the patience of the traveler. How restlessly he frets in his imprisonment! He feels the constraint like a caged hyena; his daily walk is measured by just so many feet of deck. He turns impatiently a thousand times from the staring brazen-faced binnacle (which, in the California steamers, even wants the silent companionship of the man at the helm, whose position is forward), to be met by the perpetually recurring blank wheel-house; he looks to the right, he looks to the left upon the tossing ocean; he listens to the never-ceasing creak of the timbers, and chatters his teeth in symphony with the everlasting tremor of the engine; he struggles up and tumbles down hill as the ship pitches; he staggers starboard and larboard as she rolls, until every nerve is shaken and sense confused, and the traveler hopelessly submits with a blear eye, a ringing ear, and dizzy brain to his inevitable fate.

Dinner, though no very Sybaritic enjoyment under the auspices of the improvident steward and unsavory cook of the "*Law*," was always impatiently longed for and eagerly devoured. With what restless anxiety eyes were cast through the skylights on deck, at the preparations for the great event of the day, no one but a traveler with that inexplicable voracity engendered at sea can fully comprehend. Every movement is watched, and each man feels that his fate is in the hands of Negro Dick, or Irish Patrick, as it may be; and how deliberately that inflexible fellow spreads the dirty cloth; how tediously he lengthens out expectation between the slow succession of knives and forks, clattering plates, and clinking glasses; and then, how he pauses before the hungry contemplation, until, with measured tread, he renews his slow efforts. "Now!" eagerly exclaims the beholder, and turning away angrily adds, with fretful disappointment, "d—n it, it's only the pickles!" And so, the long tedium of preliminary preparation being over, the gong roars, and the impatient crowd hurry to their knives and forks. The promise of the entertainment so brilliantly set forth in the conglomerate Franco-Hibernian of the steward's bill of fare was but meagrely sustained by the reality, nor did any one console himself more readily with a tough beef-steak, surrounded by a frozen gutter of fat, because the steward was pleased to dignify it with the elegant appellation of "*Fillet of Bœuf soused.*" The appetite, however, wonderfully overcame all obstacles, and those dinners, which are conscientiously believed to have been cooked in the ice-house, were eaten with an enjoyment that no Lucullus could give as a sauce to the choicest of his spreads ashore. Endless bottles of Champagne, fiery Sherry, and of our dearly beloved Chateaux Margaux—providently supplied by the railroad Amphitryon—cheered our party of seventeen daily, and always ended the worst of dinners in the best of humors, and sent us away rejoicing and staggering (from the motion of the ship, let it be understood) to our cigars on deck.

Thus we passed ten days, eating voraciously, drinking deeply, sleeping heavily, promenading the deck perpetually, smoking vigorously, observing each other curiously, attempting to read vainly, and yawning infinitely. The steamer, in the mean time, moved on in her course at the regular jog-trot rate of 250 miles a day, carrying us from the memorable winter of 1855 in New York (where, the New York Tribune informed us, as we read stewing in a Panama sun, that the thermometer had reached on February 7th 20° below zero), southward along the coasts of Carolina, Georgia, Florida, gradually through these milder latitudes into the Tropic of Cancer, in and out among the isles of the Caribbean Sea, giving us a passing glance of the green hills of Cuba and St. Domingo, and a glorious vision of the Blue Mountains of Jamaica, a hundred miles distant, set in the golden frame of a tropical sunset. Seething by day in the broiling heat of the perpetual summer, where Cancer holds sway and writhes its prey in its torrid grasp, and refreshed by night with the gentle fanning of the trade-winds, the staunch "*Law*," finally, on the eleventh day of the voyage, stopped her perpetual wheels, and trembling no longer under her hard struggle with the ocean, floated in like a tired sea-monster, and leaned breathless against the dock at Aspinwall.

CHAPTER II.

ASPINWALL.

APPROACHING arrival at Aspinwall was indicated by the unusual stir on board ship the day before. The baggage was hoisted up, lumbering the quarter-deck with a miscellaneous heap of multiform portmanteaus, trunks, chests, and other traveling encumbrances, and bringing together the throng of anxious owners, who hovered watchfully around their property. Great cables were coiled up by the unshipshape, greasy, steamboat men, who, with not a tarpaulin among them, in the Bowery rig of red flannel, frouzy woolen trowsers, strapped over round shoulders, and stuffed into mouldy boots, would not have been acknowledged as brother tars by any genuine Jack afloat. The steward was indefatigable that day, and proved his long latent capabilities by the last excellent dinner, in which grumbling passengers were conciliated with roast turkey, ice-cream, and plum-pudding. The negro waiters brightened themselves up with clean white jackets and affable looks, and, hopeful of coming gratuities, eagerly anticipated every call. The purser's black herald awakened each ear to his startling bell, and the announcement, "Gentlemen will please call at the purser's office and settle their wine bills!" a polite invitation, though tardily and by no means gratefully responded to. Our party agreeably appreciated on the occasion the privileges of being guests, by having no account to settle with that courteous but pertinacious purser, and scorned his grinning herald's proclamation with the cool indifference of independent gentlemen. All night the steamer groaned with noisy effort, the engine trembled with unwonted struggles, the beams creaked sharper than ever, and the heavy tramp of the busy sailors, the heaving and hoisting, the pounding of blocks, and the clanking of chains over the berths prevented sleep and disposed to early rising.

On the morning of Thursday, 16th February, I got an early glance of the land through the port-hole of my room, and hurrying up, reached the deck as the sun was rising through the gray mist of night which had exhaled from the dank verdure flooding the land, and still lingered above the thick-wooded heights of Point Manzanilla. As the steamer hurried round the Point, the bay was revealed in all the brightness of the morning sun. Just over the port bow, in the distance, low upon the surface of the water, the white houses of Aspinwall stared at us; while on either side rose the undulating heights, profusely covered with green growth from base to summit, which bound the harbor. The steamer came in from the exposed north of the bay, before the prevailing wind of the season, which was briskly stirring the sea into white crisp waves, fluttering the flag at the mast-head and our linen jackets, and tempering the lurid heat of the tropical sun.

As the steamer neared the town, the general view was dissolved into its separate details, and the eye glanced from object to object—now resting upon a native canoe bowing gracefully upon the waves, now upon a pelican diving for fish, now upon the cocoa-nut palms, which, rising with a graceful bend to the sea, from the surf-whitened beach, fluttered their feathery tops high in the air, and now upon the fleet of craft which, scattered about, swung in the swell of the harbor. And then the steamer, having skillfully bent her way through the shipping, close in, stopped her engine, and was tediously warped into dock by the aid of the hawsers now uncoiled from the deck, and laid alongside the wooden pier, facing the street of straggling, white-painted houses which border the shore. The shanty, tumble-down look of the town, in spite of the profuse proffers of entertainment, thrust, in large painted signs, upon the eyes—among which the LONE STAR shone conspicuously—did not extend a very inviting welcome to the voyager.

Nor were we eager for the embrace of those denizens of that famous town, as they stalked aboard, with their gaunt, skeleton persons clothed in white, and with ghastly death's-heads under Panama hats, and stared with ghostly wonder upon us animated beings, fresh and fat from the land of the living. The cigars they smoked so perpetually—puffing them with all their breath, as if they were the last embers of life to brighten a hope with—were the only signs of animation and proofs of human brotherhood. I thought regretfully of home, and scorned all the bitter recollections of that cold February left behind ten days before in New York, and would have gladly exchanged the dangerous delights of a tropical summer for the safe though rude discomforts of a northern winter.

The leading officials of the railroad were soon announced, and being duly presented by the dignified director who headed our party, we commenced an acquaintance which ripened at once into a hearty intimacy with some as glorious spirits (not to doubt their corporeal existence) as adorn this earth, and whose meagre frames are but scant indications of their full hearts. Under the guidance of these gentlemen, we—seventeen of the railroad party, strengthened by the addition of the American Minister to New Granada, his affable wife, and vivacious daughter—passed from ship to shore. Straggling along the wooden pier, through the gate, close by the great iron water-tanks, and the door of the steamboat agent's house and offices—cheerfully bright with white paint, and shaded by a grove of cocoa-nuts—we followed the railroad track along the front of the town, on the edge of the shore, overtaking groups of fellow-passengers who sweated in the hot sun under loads of baggage, straggled uncertainly, and inquired anxiously their way to hotels. On we went, staring at lounging, half-naked negroes, turbaned Coolies, and pale, livid white men, in Panama hats and linen jackets, until we reached the further end of the town, where our generous hosts bowed us into our welcome quarters, and refreshed us with iced claret, to which none objected except those who preferred brandy-and-water.

Our domicile was a large roomy wooden

house, double storied, with piazzas above and below, in front and rear. The whole affair, from its shingled roof to foundation, was an importation from the forests and saw-mills of Maine, and had been originally intended for a hotel, but now wisely appropriated for the use of the officials of the Panama Railroad Company; and though formerly dignified by the title of the United States Hotel, is at present known simply as the "Mess House." A prudent foresight has placed it at the extreme northern end of the town, as far away as possible from the putrefying filth of the centre of the settlement, and the malignant miasma generated by the rank vegetation inland. So it stands upon the verge of the white coral shore, where the waves of the Atlantic come roaring in and throwing their spray to the very eaves, while the seaward wind from the north blowing freshly night and day, and rustling the cocoa-nut palms, sweeps through and through the expanding balconies, the open doors, light casements, and spacious rooms, until the meagre building shivers and rattles with a perpetual ague. A grove of bananas and plantains has risen in quick growth, and intermingled with orange trees, already shades the rear from the hot sun. The botanist may turn from this indigenous profusion, and peer curiously into those tubs of earth carefully shaded beneath the piazza, and his curiosity will be rewarded by a sight of some exotic cabbages of a yellow bilious hue, which he will find more valued and cared-for than all the luscious fruit of profuse native growth.

Well, the "Mess House" was our home for the time being, and the generous concession of its courteous inmates allowed our seventeen roysterers to take possession of their comfortable quarters, giving us the full liberty of the house, breakfasting, lunching, and dining us by day, pouring down our thirsty throats dozens after dozens of Alsop's pale ale at all hours, throwing open ever-renewed boxes of the choicest cigars perpetually, and sending us to bed at night to their own cool cots. The little brisk white man from Jamaica, who was honored with the title of steward of the establishment, was always at call, and his satellites, black Tom, Dick, and Harry, obeyed without a murmur the preposterous orders of the hungriest, thirstiest, and most importunate guests who ever invaded another man's house.

The mess-table had been lengthened out to expand its hospitality to the new-comers, who were honored with the higher seats at the feast.

The chief engineer presided at one end of the board, expanding his genial welcome every where, while the chaplain fed at the other in the intervals of the grace before and after meat, when he arose to give thanks properly, but rather lengthily, for the blessings vouchsafed. Various assistant-engineers, superintendents, and clerks of the road—all with the ghastly staring eye, and pulled-molasses-candy tint of complexion which mark universally the white residents of Aspinwall—filled in the intervening places at the table. Beyond an occasional yam, plantain, or banana, or perhaps a starved chicken, there was hardly an article on the table which had not come from abroad, probably Fulton Market. The servants were negroes from Jamaica, and served with that ready obedience characteristic of the African race.

After dinner there would be a gathering on the piazza, where, in the refreshing coolness of the sea-breeze, the engineers entertained their guests with the history of their great enterprise, and submitted, with an inexhaustible good-nature, to a raking fire of questions from the anxious stockholders and inquisitorial newspaper reporters, who made up our party. And I fear that those good-natured answers led to some ill-favored results; for did not the prudent X——, by return of steamer, write to Wall Street and order a peremptory sale of all his bonds and stock? Did not the artful Y—— inform his father, in the brokerage line, that he had better metamorphose himself into a bear? Did not the truthful Z—— tell the public, as he was bound on his conscience to do, the whole truth, and nothing but the truth, and get terribly slandered and berated for having ventured upon so bold a step as to publish facts in the newspaper which employed and paid him for that purpose, which is supposed to be honorable, although it appeared otherwise to the confused conscience of the pure-minded stock-jobbers of Wall Street?

There was but little temptation at the Mess House to do much else than eat, drink, smoke, and sleep; the provision for which, it must be confessed, was of the most excellent kind. The zealous Methodist chaplain had made a praiseworthy effort to improve a taste for reading, by a generous diffusion of tracts on the hall table, with such attractive titles as, "Prepare to Die," "Will you go to Hell?" and other equally comforting suggestions; but it is feared the heathen only used them to light their cigars, or to serve a less worthy purpose.

Colon, or rather Aspinwall, as the Yankee

settlers insist upon calling it with as much propriety as if the Irishmen should, in spite of the Know Nothings, insist upon christening New York, Kilkenny or Cork, is upon the island of Manzanilla at the northeast of Navy Bay. The island is about a mile in length, and half a mile in width, extending north and south. The busy coral insect laid its foundation deep down into the depths of the sea, and is still hard at work with so much success that some fear an encroachment upon the conveniences of the harbor, though this is hardly possible in any period of time short of a geological era. Coral in all its arborescent forms can be picked up every where in abundance, together with the sponge, and many varieties of shells. The white beach which bounds the seaward edge of the island, and, in fact, the railroad track which skirts the same side of the town, are compact with the masonry of the little coral worm which had built its wonderful structures, extended its endless subterranean passages, and erected its enduring palaces long before man had thought of his clumsy pathway of iron, and his flimsy pine-board city.

A gradual accumulation of organic matter thrown up by the perpetual tide of the Atlantic, aided by the unceasing activity of the winds and birds, and then spread over the solid foundation of coral, supplied a bed of rich soil, from which sprang the rank vegetation of tropical luxuriance. A forest, centuries old, covered the island, and the spreading mangrove, the mahogany tree, and the poisonous manzanilla, interlaced with creeping vines, which hung their graceful festoons from bough to bough, overshadowed it with a perpetual shade, until civilization dispersed the dark cloud of growth impenetrable to the sun. The settlers have cleared a narrow space seaward, leaving here and there in the town the shade of a towering mangrove, or a grove of cocoa-nuts rustling upon the sea-shore, while inland the thickly-matted jungle of the manzanilla still darkens the island and exhales its poisonous breath.

The island of Manzanilla is but a few inches above the level of the Atlantic at high-tide, and being as porous as a sponge, from the nature of the soil—composed of the detritus of vegetable growth—is, consequently, with the exception of a narrow rim of coral shore, an oozy marsh. With such a soil, and a perpetual summer, the temperature of which rises to 84°, and never descends below 72°, with incessant rain six months of the year, and frequent showers during the so-called dry season—from December to June—the island is, of course, unhealthy. The alternate action of sun and rain upon the rank vegetable growth, saturated with moisture and seething in a constant summer-heat, necessarily keeps up a perpetual process of rotting fermentation, which engenders intermittent, bilious, congestive, and yellow fevers, and the other malignant results of impure miasmatic exhalation. There is, however, a constant sea-breeze during the dry season, that blows from the cool north, which tempers the heat, and somewhat mitigates the unhealthiness of the climate, by diluting the poisonous atmosphere which hangs like a pall of death over the island, and stifles the breath of human life.

The island of Manzanilla lies, near the opening, in a bend of Navy or Limon Bay, at the northeast. There is a wide expanse of sea on all but the southern side, where a narrow strait of water separates it from the mainland. The chief harbor is on the west, where the largest ships can anchor within a short distance of the shore; but such is the exposure to the fierce northers which occasionally blow, that no vessel is perfectly secure. The hazardous anchorage was sadly illustrated a short time since, when a fierce north wind blew in from the Atlantic, and swept the fleet of traders from their moorings, carrying a brig through the wooden pier, dashing a large vessel—from which no man escaped—upon the neighboring shore, and strewing the beach with wrecks, which yet remain as memorials of the fatal storm. The steamer *Illinois*, then in dock, was only saved from destruction, of which she was in great peril, by hastily firing up, letting go her hawsers, and forcing herself, with all the might of her engine, into the very teeth of the wind. The harbor will never be secure until a large breakwater is built at the northwest of the island—at the point where now a wooden bridge stretches out, with a tall look-out at the extremity, which serves as a lighthouse at night—to protect it from the fierce northers and the swell of the Atlantic, which comes sweeping all before it like a tornado. There is a roadstead on the east of the island, where there is also a considerable depth of water, but it is so little secure that it does not deserve to be termed a harbor. Sailing vessels have, in the difficulty of getting away from the island, with almost a perpetual head-wind to beat against, to pay dearly for the propitious northern gale which hurries them into port.

Navy Bay was but little known to ancient

navigators, with the exception of those bold robbers, the pirate Morgan and his men, who made it their hiding-place, whence they pounced out, with drawn hangers and blazing cannon, upon the silver-laden Spanish galleons, sailing from the neighboring Chagres and Portobello; and to modern sailors, until the adventurous American appropriators, armed with ax and shovel, commenced their march of civilization. In 1850, the engineers and laborers of the Panama Railroad Company, under the spirited leadership of the indefatigable traveler, the late John L. Stephens, with a favoring wind blowing fresh from their own northern land of vigorous enterprise, sailed into Navy Bay, and landed upon the coral beach of Manzanilla island. The forest rapidly yielded to the well-plied ax of the hardy adventurers, whose untiring labors by day soon found a rest by night under the cover of an American roof of Maine shingles. American enterprise never faltered before the terrors of a wilderness of vegetation, the growth of ages, the deep darkness of which shadowed the eye like a perpetual cloud, while the howl of the tiger from its depths startled the ear, and the pestilential breath of its jungle fevered the blood. The strong arm struck blow after blow, encouraged by the bold heart which feared neither the pestilence nor the wild blast; the resisting barriers of the overgrown wilderness gave way, and now American enterprise has stretched its iron arms across the hitherto impenetrable Isthmus of Darien, which bring together in one embrace the Atlantic and Pacific.

The town of Aspinwall, as the Atlantic terminus of the railroad, soon became the nucleus of a settlement, and at this moment rejoices in the proud distinction of a city. There are some sanguine anticipations of its future, as I discovered when the ingenious draughtsman of the Railroad Company rolled out the plan of the city, and pointed out to me, with intense enthusiasm, the great Aspinwall in future, expanding over several feet of Bristol-board, with its wide avenues, A, B, C, and so on, to the exhaustion of the whole alphabet (the numerals being brought into play for the side streets). The courteous artist—who, I fear, is too much given to the cultivation of the "ideal"—kindly led me all over the modern Carthage, through the avenues, down the cross streets, along the great docks, giving me an imaginary drive on the magnificent promenade which surrounds the city, and takes up a very large portion of the Bristol-board; and, finally, dropping me in the great central Park, left me there to rest my tired imagination. I was somewhat lost, I must confess, when, after taking leave of my good-natured, but I fear somewhat crack-brained guide, I attempted to find my way in the real city to that beautiful park and that pleasant promenade. In fact, I could not get any farther in the alphabet of the avenues than A and B, and was puzzled to count as far as number III. in the numerals. Avenue C appeared an impenetrable jungle to my confused brain; and although I had counted streets I. and II. as I passed over two wooden bridges so denominated, I could not for the world of me discover how I was to get through number III. unless, like Cæsar, I plunged into a very considerable arm of the sea which flows into the centre of the town, at the imminent hazard of drowning, and with the certainty of a tertian ague, which were the unpleasant consequences of a similar imprudence to the afore-mentioned distinguished Roman.

A hundred or so are about the whole number of houses in Aspinwall. Upon the beach at the northern end of the island are a few scattered buildings, gay with white paint and green blinds, chiefly occupied by the officials of the Panama Railroad, while to the right of these are the works and dépôt of the company with machine shops and reservoirs. The shore at the north curves round, leading easterly to an uncleared portion of the island, where a narrow rim of white beach separates the sea from the impenetrable jungle. As we turn westerly and follow the shore, taking the Mess House as the point of departure, we come upon a building of corrugated iron in progress of erection, intended for the residence of the British Consul, if he will ever have the courage to live in what is only a great target for all the artillery of heaven. The lightning during the rainy season keeps it in a continual blaze of illumination, and I mourned, in common with Colonel Totten, whose house is next door, over several prostrate cocoa-nut palms, which had been struck down in consequence of their fatal propinquity to the iron-house. As we proceed we pass three wooden, peaked-roofed cottages with green blinds and verandas, inhabited by employés of the Company; hurry past some ugly whitewashed buildings, which the pale-faced sailor and the melancholy convalescent negro, sitting smoking their pipes on the steps, remind us are hospitals, and soon passing by some outlying huts with half naked negresses and pot-bellied children sunning themselves in front, we make our way into the thicker part of the settlement over marshy pools corrupt with decaying matter, black rotten roots of trees, and all kinds of putrefying offal, which resist even the street-cleaning capacities of those famous black scavengers, the Turkey buzzards, which gather in flocks about it. We now get upon the railroad track, which leads us into the main street. A meagre row of houses facing the water made up of the railroad office, a store or two, some half dozen lodging and drinking establishments, and the "Lone Star," bounds the so-called street on one side, and the railroad track, upon its embankment of a few feet above the level of the shore, bounds the other.

There is another and only one other street, which you reach by crossing a wooden bridge, that a sober man can only safely traverse by dint of deliberate care in the day-time, and a drunken man never, and which stretches over a large sheet of water that ebbs and flows in the very centre of the so-called city. This second street begins at the coral beach at the northern end of the island, and runs southward until it terminates in a swamp. At the two extremities houses bound it on both sides; in the middle there is a narrow pathway over an insecure foot-bridge, with some tumble down pine buildings on one side only, with their foundations soaking in the swamp, their back windows inhaling the malaria from the manzanilla jungle in the rear, and their front ones opening upon the dirty water which we have already described that fills up the central part of the city. The hotels—great, straggling, wooden houses—gape here with their wide open doors, and catch California travelers, who are sent away with a fever as a memento of the place, and shops, groggeries, billiard-rooms, and drinking saloons thrust out their flaring signs to entice the passer-by. All the houses in Aspinwall are wooden with the exception of the stuccoed Railroad office, the British Consul's precarious corrugated iron dwelling, and a brick building in the course of erection under the slow hands of some Jamaica negro masons. The more pretentious of the wooden buildings were sent out from Maine or Georgia bodily, and among them is the largest building in the place, the United States Hotel, which belongs to a Mr. Aspinwall of New York, and which I was sorry to hear does not pay.

The inhabitants of Aspinwall—some eight hundred in number—are of every variety of race and shade in color. The railroad officials, steamboat agents, foreign consuls, and a score of Yankee traders, hotel-keepers, billiard markers, and bar-tenders, comprise all the whites, who are the exclusive few. The better class of shop-keepers are Mulattoes from Jamaica, St. Domingo, and the other West Indian Islands, while the dispensers of cheap grog, and hucksters of fruit and small wares are chiefly negroes. The main body of the population is made up of laborers, grinning coal-black negroes from Jamaica, yellow natives of mixed African and Indian blood, and sad, sedate, turbaned Hindoos, the poor exiled Coolies from the Ganges.

The arrival of the Californian passengers from New York or Panama each fortnight is a great event at Aspinwall. The population is doubled at once by the new-comers, who, arriving from New York and San Francisco, often meet together in the town, and exchange greetings from the two oceans. The inanimate lethargy of the place is at once quickened by the stirring adventurers. The hotels, deserted the day before as empty packing-boxes, are thronged, and mine hosts, awakened once more to the consciousness of their functions of taking in people; bar-rooms again reek with an atmosphere of gin-sling and brandy-cock-tail, which the now busy, bilious-faced bar-keeper, only yesterday prostrate with fever, shuffles across the counter in a quick succession of drinks to his throng of impatient, thirsty customers; billiard balls, long stowed away in pockets, begin to circulate, driven by the full force of sturdy, red flannel-sleeved arms; the shops flutter out in the breeze their displays of Panama hats and loose linen garments, and adding a hundred per cent. to their prices, do a brisk business; the very monkeys quicken their agility, the parrots chatter with redoubled loquacity, the macaws shriek sharper than ever, the wild hogs, ant-eaters, and even the sloths (for all these zoological varieties abound in the houses, hotels, and shops of Aspinwall) are aroused to unwonted animation.

Apart from the devoted family of the agent of the Atlantic steamers, by whose refined and generous hospitality I was consoled for the absence of home, there is no society blessed by the gentle and holy influence of cultivated woman. The natural consequence of this want of the most powerful, since it is the most resistless, social tie, is a wild recklessness of life, which startles one subdued, if not entirely subjected, by the obligations of a more conventional society. While the residents of Aspinwall are the freest, frankest, and most hospitable of men, it can not be denied that a little more constraint, however it might stifle and restrict their generous qualities, would improve their health and not injure their morals. There was a perpetual excitement among those men I met, which may be partly attributed to the excessive nervous sensibility engendered by the climate and its diseases; but I am sure it was increased by their habits. I do not wish to affect the Puritan, nor do I care that the reader should suppose that I am now, or ever, in a very penitent mood; but I will at this moment both profess and confess. I profess the belief that drinking Champagne cock-tails before breakfast, and smoking forty cigars daily, to be an immoderate enjoyment of the good things of this world. Now, by the way of a *peccavi*, I will make a clean breast of it, by acknowledging that I, in common with my Aspinwall friends, did both.

Now let the uncharitable reader pause before he condemns me. Hear, oh ye civilized Pharisee! It was hot—remember I was writhing in the grasp of the torrid crab—I was thirsty, and drink I must. "Well," you coolly interpose, "take a glass of water." "Thank you!

a glass of pure Croton with all my heart," I answer; "but the Croton pipes are not yet laid as far as Aspinwall, and the tanks of rain-water, the only supply in that delectable city, are stagnant and fever-and-aguish." "What shall I drink?" I asked the friend at my side. "A Champagne cock-tail—the most delicious thing in the world—let me make you one," was his response; and he suited the action to the word. A bottle of prime, sparkling "Mum" was brought, a refreshing plateful of crystal ice, fresh from Rockland by the last steamer, and rather a medicinal looking bottle, upon which was written in direct, brief terms, "Bitters." My friend, whose benevolent eyes expressed pity for my sufferings, while his lips were eloquent of prospective alleviation to myself, and of consciousness, the result of long experience, of his own anticipated enjoyment, pounded the crystal ice, with a series of quick, successive blows, pattered it into the tumblers like a shower of hail, dropped in the bitters, which diffused a glow like that of early sunrise, dashed in the sugar, which somewhat clouded the beautiful prospect, and gave what the artists call a dead tint to the mixture; then out popped the eager "Mum," and the Champagne cock-tail, thus perfected, went whirling, roaring, foaming, and flowing down mine and the friendly concocter's thirsty throats. I have preached my sermon, and illustrated it by my own bad example, from which the reader may take warning, and not taste Champagne cock-tails, for they are so supremely good that if he once takes them, he will continue to take them, and not take the former.

I say nothing by way of protest against the frequent practice of drinking *quinine* cock-tails, in which quinine is substituted for bitters, and the by no means agreeable but constant habit of freely indulging in quinine pills; for these are excusable, if not necessary on the score of health. It is a melancholy fact, that such is the unhealthiness of Aspinwall, that its inhabitants are obliged to mix medicine with their daily drink, and to pass around their pill-boxes with the frequency of a French snuff-taker of the ancient régime. I have been seriously invited, time and again, to drink a quinine cock-tail, and to help myself out of a proffered box, to a pill or two, which, I need not say, I politely declined.

I had no reason to go into the hospitals, which I did, and saw some miserable specimens of suffering humanity, to find out the state of health in Aspinwall. A walk in the streets was painfully convincing of the fact that I was among the sick and the dying. The features of every man, woman, or child, European, African, Asiatic, or American, I met had the ghastly look of those who suffer from the malignant effects of miasmatic poison. I do not believe there is a wholesome person in all Aspinwall; at any rate, every single individual I asked confessed to having suffered from the disease of the climate. The little negro Jamaica children invariably answered my question as to how they liked the country, with the plaintive words, "Me no like dis country, berra bad country; me hab de feber ebry oder day." A physician employed by the Railroad Company, who has been two years on the Isthmus, told me plainly that no one who resided over two months in Aspinwall escaped fever; that the first attack was generally a severe bilious remittent, which not seldom resulted in death, and was always followed by habitual fever and ague. Such, he assured me, was the intense malignity of the miasmatic poison, that perfect recovery from the disease of the climate, or any acclimation, unless a perpetual fever and ague may be so termed, was impossible. The beasts even do not escape. That hardiest of animals, the mule, is a frequent sufferer, and

I made the acquaintance of a poor Newfoundland dog that was a martyr to the universal complaint.

Aspinwall and its neighborhood, though abounding in causes destructive of life, are very deficient in the necessaries for its support. A scant supply of drinking water is obtained by collecting the rain in large iron tanks, which as yet are so few that the inhabitants are forced to send to Gatun, several miles distant, to satisfy their wants. The chief articles of food come from the New York market, although the neighboring coasts supply a few fowls and a small quantity of the tropical fruits and vegetables. Canoes occasionally arrive with melons, green cocoanuts, pines, yams, and oranges, and a sparse market of these is displayed on the shore by the Indian hucksters, who have become, under the civilizing influences of Aspinwall, tolerably sharp at a bargain. Fish must abound in the bay, but there seems to have been little development as yet of this resource. Milk is obtained from the goats, which are seen picking up a scanty subsistence from the refuse vegetable garbage in the town.

Having packed my portmanteau, I paid the

following washing bill, which will show that a fair day's labor receives a fair day's wages in Aspinwall:

ASPINWALL.

—— ——

To *Charlotte Miles.*

February 23, 1855.

To washing twenty-four pieces wearing apparel at 20 cents each.................................... $4 80

Charlotte Miles, whom I had never the pleasure of seeing in person, as she did her business with me through her negro proxy, Sam of the Mess House, might have become the owner in perpetuity of my stockings, for washing each one of which she charged twenty cents, at the tenth of the sum a pair, and she would have had no bargain at that. Charlotte Miles having received her money, I prepared to leave Aspinwall for Panama.

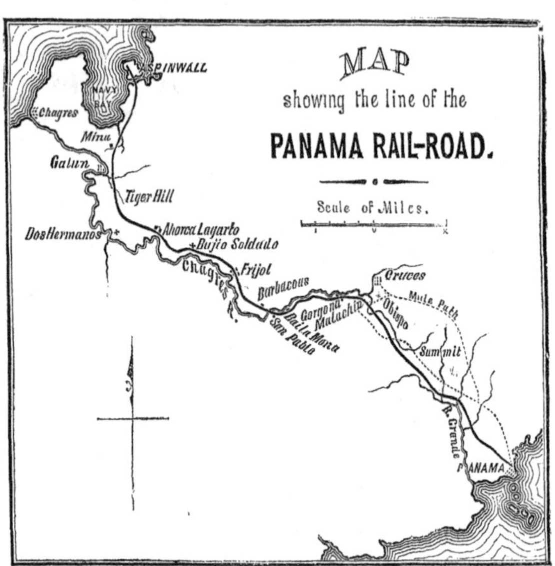

CHAPTER III.

RIDE ON THE RAILROAD.

I WAS pleased when it was announced, in accordance with the projected programme of the entertainment of our party on the Isthmus, that we were to take an early departure from that plague-spot, Aspinwall. That disease and premature death were endemic in that region of swamp and vegetable rottenness, was quite evident without any minute investigation into the topographical characteristics of a city, the foundation of which is below the level of the Atlantic, and every breath of its air charged with the poisonous exhalation of vegetable decay. There was no need to investigate the physical causes which, in accordance with the laws of health, must lead to the deadly effects of malignant disease. There was no necessity of studying the statistics, which are but a continuous record of death, when the ghastly face of every man you met was a *memento mori*. It is not only the American white man who wilts, decays, and dies, in the malignant atmosphere, which is the breath of death and not of life, inspired by the inhabitant of Aspinwall.

The people of all countries, and of all races and color, whom the call of duty, the stimulus of enterprise, and the hard necessities of labor have gathered together in Aspinwall, are equally forced to pay the fatal tribute demanded by the inexorable fate which overshadows with its dark wings that region, and strikes down every one prostrate in resistless acknowledgment of its terrible tyranny. The hearty and energetic Caucasian from Europe and the United States, the temperate Asiatic, the tropical African, and the phlegmatic native Indian, are alike subjected to the terrors of that land of the pestilence. When, therefore, on the morning of February 18, the shrill sound of the steam-whistle, piercing through the open door, and the rattling casements of the "Mess House," aroused us with its familiar note of preparation, and startled the voracious buzzards, which were disputing eagerly with decay, the carrion washed up by the waves of the Atlantic to our very door, there was not one of us who did not gladly welcome the token of departure.

The seventeen who composed our party were a miscellaneous gathering of stockholders, young lawyers, men about town, and newspaper reporters, headed by a director of the Railroad Company. It had been resolved in Congress assembled, of the Board of Directors at New York, that the opening of the road from the Atlantic to the Pacific was an occasion that ought not to be allowed to pass unimproved. It was undoubtedly a great, a very great occasion, and should be celebrated with becoming éclat. The enthusiasm of the public required to be stimulated, as was clearly proven by the fact that the stock stagnated in Wall Street at the dead level of par, when, if justly appreciated, it could not fail to rise to a premium of 50 per cent. at the lowest calculation.

Europe, too, was either in a state of profound ignorance of its own interests, or in such a complete dead-lock at Sebastopol, that it was felt necessary to disperse the financial clouds in that country, and quicken enterprise with an electrical shock from the brisk battery of American energy. The proposal to borrow a million or so, which had been generously tendered to the London bankers, that they might be made sharers with their American brethren in the profits of the great enterprise, was not responded to in the same free spirit with which it had been proffered, and it was determined that reluctant Threadneedle Street should be aroused to a more lively sense of its own interest, as far as Panama bonds were concerned.

Accordingly, it having been resolved that the world should be shaken out of its apathetic indifference to the Panama Railroad, the directors selected a worthy representative of their board to beat up recruits for a triumphant march across the Isthmus, and to lay in supplies of Champagne, rounds of beef, pickled oysters, and other necessary stores for the expedition. If old Marshal Saxe was correct in the dogma that "he was the best general who fed his soldiers best," the company had no reason to regret their appointment of one who worthily answered the expectation of all in this very important particular.

Some notabilities of the bar and the pulpit, and various loquacious members of Congress, and other dignitaries, were urged to blow their trumpets on the occasion; but they refused, either from a prudent dislike to Panama fever, or because "their engagements prevented them from taking part in the interesting celebration of the great occasion of the union of the two oceans," which they, of course, "deeply regretted." The worthy director, therefore, disappointed of the magnates, made up his party, like the rich man in the parable, of the first he met; so we seventeen were not a distinguished company, though a respectable one nevertheless.

A programme had been carefully deliberated upon during the voyage. The happy accident of the presence of no less a personage than the Minister to New Granada, was shrewdly turned to the advantage of the occasion. His felicity of speech, practiced in the diffuse school of congressional oratory, secured us abundant words for every occasion, and his official importance gave the necessary emphasis to all he said. He was put down at once for the oration at the laying of the corner-stone of the memorial in honor of the projectors of the Panama Railroad, and his ready eloquence appropriated for other parts in the programme. The young lawyers not unwillingly consented to perform at the projected banquet, and showed a commendable diligence in studying up their various subjects, writing their speeches over and over, giving a fresh polish to their rhetoric at each renewed effort, and finally rehearsing them so often to a select audience, among which I was a favored listener, that they could, and did, repeat them a hundred times a day without faltering in a single word. One of the reporters for the press kindly anticipated a call upon him, by generously volunteering to do duty for himself and others, and subsequently suffered a martyrdom on his legs, which called out the sympathy of the public in general, and his brethren in particular.

The especial object of our journey by the railroad was to put into execution what had been so elaborately prepared. All the Isthmus was in a state of excited anticipation of the event, and the performers on the occasion were no less moved. The Minister to Nicaragua ruminated his tobacco cud with unusual nervous agitation, and kept a brisk look-out for his morocco portfolio, big with his swelling oratory;

and the other aspiring orators were eager to break the eggs of their eloquence, which had been so long in a state of incubation, and anxious to try themselves as newly-fledged Demosthenes within the sound of the roar of the Pacific.

Aspinwall was in a state of unusual stir on the morning of our departure. All the stars and stripes in the town and harbor had been unfurled at an early hour, and were fluttering in the sea-breeze from every roof and mast-head. The hotels and drinking-saloons were gay with their bits of bunting. The Negro laborers were intensely enthusiastic on the occasion, and came out in great force. Some making carnival in grotesque disguises, and all grinning their white ivories and shouting vociferously. The melancholy Coolies, who leaned their turbaned heads against the corners of the houses, or reclined in graceful attitudes beneath the shade of the balconies, were alone silent and unmoved. A party of Jamaica Negroes had got possession of a rusty cannon, and kept firing it with the glee of so many boys on a holiday. Their shouts of merriment went ringing through the crowd, when of a sudden the joyful hurra was turned into a shriek of woe. A Negro, who was loading the cannon, was struck with the rammer from the premature discharge of the piece, in consequence of the man whose duty it was to assist him having lifted his finger from the vent. We left the poor fellow surrounded by a throng of wailing Negroes, prostrate on the ground, insensible from the concussion of the blow, and with the flesh torn from his face. We learned subsequently that he died.

The passengers for California gathered from the various hotels throughout the town, where they had been detained a night, much to their discontent, and now thronged in a noisy crowd about the Railroad office bargaining for bananas, green cocoa-nuts, and oranges, with the Jamaica Negro-women, who went in and out among the gathered groups, poising their loaded baskets upon their heads, eagerly pressing their merchandise upon their chaffering customers, with their glossy, ebony faces spread out into an expansive grin, which showed their teeth glistening large, white, and regular as the keys of a piano set in rosewood, or chattering angrily with each other in amusing negro talk. The bell rang, the engine, which had been impatiently moving to and fro, sprang to its place, the passengers thronged into the cars, and with a shrill whistle, a shout from the miscellaneous crowd gathered in the street, and a wave of the handkerchief from a solitary white woman in the upper balcony of the "Lone Star," we were off.

Emerging from the long sheds of the railroad dépôt car after car, the train briskly moved along the street with its meagre row of buildings on the left, which fell one after the other from the eye, and passed away rapidly in the distance like a scud of thin white cloud. So, too, on the right, quickly disappeared the harbor and its little fleet of coasters, the Steamship Company's long wooden pier and offices, showing whiter in the bright morning sun, and in deeper contrast than ever with the green cocoa-nut grove, and the great black hull of the steamer; so, too, for a moment only, the bright surface of the bay glittered on the eye, as the train passed along the shore of the island across the inlet, and plunged into the depths of the forest.

As we lounged at our ease in the well-appointed New Jersey car, and smoked, and talked, and looked with admiring wonder upon the tropical profusion of beauty, which every turn of the road revealed to the view, it was difficult to appreciate the enterprise, the skill, the labor, and the suffering, which had been so prodigally expended in effecting what came to us only in the shape of comfort and enjoyment. How rapidly we glided mile after mile, and so smoothly, that the ashes were not shaken from the cigar we were smoking in such comfortable contentment, and yet there was hardly a foot of the way which was not a prodigy of laborious enterprise. The town we had left was, but five years ago, a forest, and the pathway a jungle. Enterprise had struck down the one, and made its resolute march through the other.

For seven miles the road passes through a deep marsh, in which the engineers, during the original survey, struggled breast-high, day after day, and yet, in spite of such toilsome and perilous labor, fixed their steady eyes straight forward, went on step by step, and accomplished their purpose. These seven miles are firm now as a stone pavement. Piles upon piles have been driven deep down into the spongy soil, and the foundation covered thick with a persistent earth, brought from Monkey Hill, which overhangs the railroad track two miles from Aspinwall.

On we go, dry shod, over the marsh, through the forest, which shuts out with its great walls of verdure on either side, the hot sun, and darkens the road with a perpetual shade. The luxuriance of the vegetation is beyond the powers of description. Now we pass impenetrable thickets of mangroves, rising out of deep marshes, and sending from each branch down into the earth, and from each root into the air, offshoots which gather together into a matted growth, where the observer seeks in vain to unravel the mysterious involution of trunk, root, branch, and foliage. Now we come upon gigantic *espaves* and *coratos*, with girths of thirty feet, and statures of a hundred and thirty feet, out of a single trunk of which, without a plank or a seam, the natives build great vessels of twelve tons burden. These giants of the forest seem, like the Titans, offspring of heaven and earth, for they embrace with their mighty arms the one, and cling deep down into the bosom of the other; and the great twining plants which, rising from their roots, coil about their trunks, bind themselves in twisted fibre about their branches, and joining these great trees inseparably together, fasten them to the ground, remind us of the imprisonment which the Titans of old suffered from the cruelty of their father, Cœlus.

Again we cross a stream, rippling between banks of verdant growth, where the graceful bamboo waves over the water its feathery top, and the groves of the vegetable ivory palm, intermingled with the wild fig-tree, spread their shade, and rustling gently in the breeze, whisper a slight murmur of solitude in the ear, and suggest a passing dream of repose.

Then, again, the train coiling its winding way about the base of a hill, and emerging from the forest, the view opens suddenly upon an expanded savanna, where the tropical sun shines down in a flood of light upon a river bending through an undulating park of green verdure, with clumps of trees here and there, with cattle feeding in their shade, and a settlement of native, palm-thatched, bamboo huts, half hid in groves of banana and orange. So we hurry from scene to scene, pushing on through the flood of tropical vegetation, with endless vistas of beauty that come and go like the dreams of a summer's day. But we must proceed more deliberately.

Gatun, seven miles from Aspinwall, was our first stopping-place, where we rested for a moment, that the newspaper reporters might have an opportunity of taking note of the expression of the enthusiasm of the Gatun officials and laborers, on the occasion of the day's celebration. Accordingly, I read afterward in the *Journal of Commerce*, or in some other of the equally poetical papers diurnally served up with our morning coffee, that we passed under "a triumphal arch, where the graceful palm, entwined with the brilliant flowers of the Isthmus, waved over our heads." I recollect having seen, on the top of a clay bank, in front of a Maine house of pine boards, partly falling into decay, one white man, two Negroes, and a Cooly, who were shouting at the top of their voice, and firing off a blunderbuss between them, the report of which I heard distinctly, for it flashed almost in my face as I passed, and seemed to go off with accumulative force, probably from being loaded and fired by four men.

At Gatun station the railroad comes close to the right bank of the Chagres, and keeps it for twelve miles or so, during which there is an occasional view of the tortuous course of the river, always upon the right of the traveler facing Panama. From the Gatun station we saw the native village of that name, with its huts scattered on the opposite bank of the Chagres, facing the mouth of the river Gatun. Many of the dusky inhabitants, the men in clean, white linen jackets and Panama hats, and the women in loose gowns, weighed down with cotton fringe, which revealed their dark figures to the waist, had crossed from the village to the opposite bank, and stood at the side of the train in full holiday-glee, shouting as it passed.

Thence the train steamed away again through the tropical forest, stopping here and there to feed the engine with wood, which lay in piles along the route, or to take in water from the wooden tanks, which already were blackened with decay, and overgrown with vines of the convolvulus, gay with its blue bell-shaped flowers. I was surprised at the rarity of blossoms in the rich profusion of tropical growth. I saw but few varieties: a yellow flower growing upon a lofty spreading forest tree, some white lilies brought out in bright relief from the thick surface of green which mantled the marshes, and abundant crimson-blossomed spikes, which protruded from the dark caverns of verdure on either side like enormous red tongues of tired monsters lolling out and cooling in the fresh air.

We caught a rapid glance of the Carthagenian native laborers of the yellow mixed blood of the Spaniard, Negro, and Indian, cutting down with their machetas the wild banana, and the other thick undergrowth which the cars brushed as they passed. The sturdy Jamaica Negroes in throngs were plying the pick and the spade, in company with the turbaned, lithe-limbed

Coolies, who were lending an indolent hand, and an occasional Chinese, who might be seen loitering lazily by the roadside.

From Gatun, diverging a mile or so from the river Chagres on the right, passing Tiger Hill on the left—where if there are any tigers we did not see one, nor did we even see the tail of a monkey, or hear the chatter of a parrot, for the steam-whistle has frightened every thing but man into the deep hiding-places of the forest—coming up to the bank of the river again at Ahorca Lagarto, we reached Bujio Soldado. Here, on a green bank situated at a bend of the Chagres, which doubles and doubles upon itself a thousand times during its tortuous course, is a picturesque rustic cottage, thatched with palm, and shaded with vines and a grove of bananas. Its balconies in the rear look up and down the river, which forms an elbow at this point, and the beholder sees a wide expanse of water that reflects the deep shade of the tropical forest, which crowds up the banks of the Chagres from the water's edge far inland into the remote depths of the luxuriant wilderness. The cottage was the favorite residence of John L. Stephens the traveler, and here he enjoyed those intervals of repose which his energetic devotion to, and his untiring activity in, the railroad enterprise but rarely allowed him.

The train moves on, passing through the settlement of Frijol with its scattered huts, its sparse patches of maize and sugar-cane, and its score of half-naked natives, until it reaches Barbacoas, where the engine checks its course and crosses with deliberate care the great wooden bridge which spans the Chagres, and leads the railroad track to the left bank of that river. The bridge is 600 feet in length, and is of American pine, brought by a curious conjunction of the old and the new, from Darien in Georgia. Solid masonry supports the bridge; and the great timbers of the wooden superstructure, bound together with iron girders, look as if they might endure for ages, but alas! in that destructive climate they will be in ruin in a short twelve months. West of Barbacoas, on the right of the traveler looking Panama-ward, rises the Cierro Gigante, the loftiest eminence of the Isthmus, from which Nunez de Balboa first saw, in one glance, the Pacific and Atlantic; and as he rapturously gazed upon the two oceans, separated by the narrow Isthmus, which was diminished in his elevated view to a mere handful of earth, felt like a conqueror, and glowed with the conviction that the whole world was within his grasp.

We have now the Chagres on the left, and pass through the forest, which rarely permits a view of the dark waters of the river, except here and there, where the cleared space of a settlement on its banks, as for example the village of Gorgona, along which the railroad track is laid, gives passage to the sun, and discloses the stream sparkling in its light. Leaving Gorgona and its group of thatched huts, with their moist palm-leaf eaves, distilling clouds of vapor in the hot sun, its groves of oranges and bananas ripening in the noonday heat, and its yellow-faced inhabitants swinging in their grass hammocks, or indolently lolling in the shade, we plunge again into the forest, and thence in a moment out upon the open savanna, where we reach Matachin.

On arriving at Matachin, which is seven miles from Barbacoas, and thirty-five from Aspinwall, the train stopped, and our party, which had been increased at Aspinwall by the addition of various railroad officials, steamboat agents, and other dignitaries, and honored with a special car, the last of ten, bright and fresh from the Yankee factory, alighted, headed by the American Minister with his portentous morocco portfolio, alternately borne by her excellency, the Plenipotentiary's wife, and his vivacious daughter, who accompanied him. The passengers for California thronged out after us, presenting the usual characteristics of dare-devil manners, and free-and-easy costume, and went roystering about in slouched hats, red shirts, and heavy boots, disturbing the stillness of the hills with their noisy shouts.

It will be recollected that the chief purpose of our journey was to lay the corner-stone of a memorial in honor of the three original projectors of the Panama Railroad—J. L. Stephens, Aspinwall, and Chauncey. The spot chosen for the future monument, is the summit of one of a series of natural mounds, which, from their regularity of form, and their smooth acclivities of perpetual verdure, where the sensitive plant, interspersed with yellow flowers, shrinks from the tread, have the appearance of artificial formation. The ground undulates in these regular hills in the centre of an amphitheatre of distant mountains. Palm-trees surround their base, and wave gracefully in the breeze, which tempers the heat of the noonday tropical sun.

The scene which opened on our view, as we stood upon the mound, was magnificent, even in comparison with the tropical beauty we had already reveled in. A park-like expanse of level land stretched away on one side, with spreading trees here and there of the India rubber and of the mangrove, with herds of cattle feeding on the rich pasture; on the other, there was the palm-thatched bamboo cottage of a planter, the owner of the ground, and who, with his garden, the orange-trees of which were thrusting their golden fruit into his windows, his herds of cattle, his fields of maize and of sugar-cane, has reason to congratulate himself upon his thriving condition, as also upon the beauty in the bosom of which he reposes. In the distance the scene was closed in by mountains, from the heights and through the valleys of which floods of green verdure came pouring down until they overflowed the banks of the Chagres and Obispo, which rivers unite their waters at Matachin, and flow calmly in the shade under the overhanging foliage, or hurry rapidly in the centre current from the bright glances of the sun.

The palms which surrounded the base of the mound on which we stood were rustling in the breeze, and through their moving foliage we could see the railroad train with its engine, which was throwing out in the wind its flowing banner of steam, as if to indicate that it had subjected the land to its universal dominion. Two sturdy Negroes came toiling up with the great corner-stone, and having made their way through the crowd, which gathered about the Summit, the United States Plenipotentiary opened the morocco portfolio and delivered himself of his oration, about which I need say nothing here, for the orator providently made a dozen copies or so, and generously distributed them to the New York papers, where no doubt all my readers have carefully enlightened themselves. I fear all the company were not very close listeners to the Plenipotentiary's oratory, for, as the steam-whistle hurried us down the hill, I could see that some had taken the occasion to forage about the neighboring country, and were loaded with oranges and bananas and other tempting plunder.

We were now off again, and a cold collation having been prepared for the travelers in the special car, we had a jolly scramble for the sandwiches, olives, and pickles, which we washed down with ever-flowing draughts of Champagne and brandy-and-water. I did not see, it must be confessed, with very clear eyes the next station, Obispo, or listen with a very intelligent apprehension to all the General—a military gentleman of renown belonging to Car-

THE SUMMIT, PANAMA RAILROAD.

thagena, who, among his other deeds inscribed upon the roll of fame, I recollect that he was the first to introduce the vegetable ivory of his country into Europe—who sat next to me, had to say about Cruces, which we had passed some two miles to the left of the route, opposite Matachin. Cruces, however, is now obsolete under the railroad dispensation, though it will be always memorable in the early history of the emigration of the gold-seekers to California. It was there that the traveler first took to mule on his way to Panama, during the pouring rainy season of the Isthmus, though in the dry it was at Gorgona, farther down the river. A mule-path, once paved, said to have been built by Pizarro, leads in a break-neck, helter-skelter course up the hills and down the hills, through the narrow gorges, and across the muddy streams from Cruces to Panama, and is a hard day's ride.

Seven miles' steaming from Matachin brought us to Culebra, the Summit, as the railroad people call it, since it is the highest point on the route, being 250 feet above high tide of the Pacific. We had thus been struggling up hill from Aspinwall at the degree of ascent of 61 feet per mile, and, once at the top, we were compensated by the more rapid descent to Panama of 70 feet per mile. Here had been the heaviest work on the line, where a mass of earth, 1300 feet in length and 24 feet in depth, containing 30,000 feet in all, had been cut through to make way for the lords of creation, who were now so triumphantly speeding onward in what we are pleased to term, in spite of bowie-knives and revolvers, the march of civilization. All these entertaining statistics were communicated to me by the superintendent of the road, as he lighted his cigar by mine, and can be depended upon, for I noted them down at the moment for the especial behoof of the matter-of-fact reader. There are other cuttings on the route of no considerable depth, however, and we had passed between banks of clay and walls of columnar basalt, and through quarries of a gray freestone, out of which the stone abutments of the bridges and other masonry had been constructed, all of which were already softened to the eye by the verdure of hanging plants and clinging creepers, which grow with such miraculous rapidity in the fertile soil of the Isthmus. The embankment at the Summit is of a loose soil, and so close that we could almost touch it from the cars, and hundreds of black and yellow laborers were busy in throwing back the earth which the first shower softens, washes down, and sweeps across the track, greatly to the obstruction of travel and the successful progress of the railroad enterprise.

At the Summit, on either side of the track, there is an irregular line of some forty or so whitewashed shanties and bamboo huts, among which "Old Joe Prince's" groggery, with its staring, painted sign, stands conspicuous. Here, a few months ago, was the terminus of the railroad, where passengers alighted in the mud, and refreshing themselves with bad brandy at "Old Joe Prince's," or in some of the other delectable retreats for the tired traveler, took either to mule or railroad-car, as they were going from or to Panama. Now Culebra, or the Summit, as it is oftener called, is but a railway-station where the traveler barely has time to snuff the gin-reeking atmosphere of the groggery, or to wet his lips across "Old Joe Prince's" slushy bar.

Dark women, in Panama hats and loose drapery, came thronging about the windows of the cars as we stopped, and supplied us generously with oranges, bananas, and pineapples, at a price that we would have refused to pay in New York. A half-dozen oranges cost me the better part of a dollar; but I thought them cheap as I regaled myself with their juicy freshness, parched as I was with the exciting ride, and baked dry by the tropical sun, which was now darting its red-hot rays through the windows, and scorching the cover of the car. The oranges had a green, unripe look, like all I ate in the country, and a smooth, tight-bound skin, as if they had been plucked too soon from the mellowing touch of the sun; but as I plunged my dry mouth into their inmost depths and drew up their fountains of juice, I felt a torrent of cool liquid sweetness pouring down my thirsty throat, invigorating me with its refreshing moisture, and stimulating me with its aromatic taste. I never ate such oranges as those of Panama: they are the juiciest, the sweetest, the coolest, and the best-flavored of any that ever turned their golden globes to a tropical sun.

Just as we were about starting there waddled into our special car a native mahogany-colored woman, who did not seem at all conscious, half-barbarian as she was, of the civilized distinction of white and black, and, in spite of her Negro blood, looked as proud as the best of us. She wore a fine Panama hat, from beneath which squirmed two long twists of black shining wool; loose white drapery, trimmed with cotton lace flounces above instead of below, enveloped the lower part of her person, while the upper was naked almost to the waist; a necklace, in which American eagles plentifully abounded, connected together by golden chains, hung around her ebony throat as the Oriental women adorn themselves with sequins, and her toes were just squeezed into bright-red satin slippers, which gave a freshly-bitten, raw-meat look to her splay, unstockinged feet, which projected behind in all their full proportion of wholesome Negro heel. Captain S—— of our party, who prided himself upon his gallantry, soon crowded himself alongside of this Isthmian belle, and in a very few minutes the gallant skipper had more than his fair share of the seat, while his companion grinned her white teeth, and wagged her tails of wool with infinite laughter. The Captain insisted afterward, confidentially, that it was a decided conquest; but I shrewdly suspect that it was the worthy navigator's Spanish, which was not certainly of the purest Castilian, and not his personal attractions, or his wit, which had almost dislocated those grinning jaws and shaken off those tails of wool.

An old acquaintance, Don Carlos Z——, whom I had recollected in olden time, as a sedate merchant in Panama, with quill pacifically poised upon his ear, now came in, all whiskered like a Pandoor, with his mustaches stretching out audaciously beneath a slouched brigand hat, and his broad frame flaming with a red flannel coat, and his girdle stuck full with knives and revolvers. He told us, over a pinch of his snuff, in a few clipped words—as was always his matter-of-fact business-like manner—that he had withdrawn from the more pacific retirement of the counting-room, and having been installed Captain of the ragged Railroad Guard, now roamed over the Isthmus to the terror of all evil-doers. With this addition to our company we started again, and turned scornfully and rapidly away from "Old Joe Prince's" and his by-no-means respectable-looking neighborhood of irregular, tottering taverns and groggeries, which seemed to be much the worse for liquor, and appeared to be staggering fast down the hill of ruin and of Culebra together. The settlement at the Summit does little credit to American civilization; it is, in fact, but a rag torn from her skirts in the course of her helter-skelter progress through the wilderness.

Now we shoot rapidly down the slope eleven miles to Panama, through the forests again and out upon the Savannas, until we come within a few miles of the end of the route, where we slide easily along a level and open country to the Pacific, the sight of whose broad bosom, heaving and panting in the sun, is welcomed with shouts of delight as the train coils in among the cocoa-nut palms, and stops at the Playa Prieta on the very verge of the shore. Our watches tell us we have been only four hours and a half in making the transit of forty-eight miles from ocean to ocean. A steamer, with its great black hull rolling in the swell of the bay in the distance, some two miles off, was awaiting the arrival of the passengers for California, and as I alighted, before I had fairly shaken the stiffness out of my legs after my long ride, I could see our fellow-travelers, in red flannel, crowding down to the beach, with their blankets strapped over their shoulders, and, followed by troops of native orange-women, and naked ebony lads, springing into the boats, which leaped as lively as a shoal of fish in the surf, ready to bear the eager crowd to the distant ship.

Our party straggled on past the barn-like railroad-offices, through the neighboring settlement of bamboo huts, with their noisy swarm of yellow natives; thence along the rough, shelving shore, where we caught a glance of the boats making their way, one after another, to the steamer, like a line of floating pelicans. We continued our way through a part of the suburbs of Panama, past the provision shops, where festoons of beef hung by the yard over the doors, drying in the sun, and bags of meal, and of dried beans, with calabashes piled with red peppers, and palm-leaf baskets heaped with oranges, crowded the entrances, while the lazy proprietors, with tawny skins, swayed in hammocks in the dark shade inside, and their swarming families of naked piccaninies dabbled in the dirt, and sported in the gutters which stagnated in the centre of the street. Then we stumbled along the irregular paved way—never repaired since the days of Pizarro—over the mouldy stone bridge, green with verdure, which arches the trench, now filled with rank tropical growth, and passed through the dilapidated stone gate within the ruined walls of the city of Panama. With a few turns along the narrow streets, dark with the shadows of the projecting balconies, which nearly touched from opposite sides, we reached our destination, and were soon lounging at our ease in the cool spaciousness of the great naked rooms of the Aspinwall House.

PACIFIC TERMINUS OF PANAMA RAILROAD.

CHAPTER IV.

THE RAILROAD CONSIDERED.

I WILL here interrupt the narrative of the personal adventures of our party with a record of some facts I learned during my visit to the Isthmus, in regard to the important enterprise of the Panama Railroad.

The locomotive first passed from ocean to ocean on the 27th January, 1855, conveying the Chief Engineer, Colonel Totten, and some of his coadjutors—a triumphant result of which these men of skill and enterprise reaped the first fruition, as to them belonged the glory. The trains have run with more or less regularity ever since, securing to the traveler the comforting assurance, that he can reasonably hope to pass from the Atlantic to the Pacific, and from the Pacific to the Atlantic in the short period of little more than four hours, with all the facility and comfort that the same space may be traversed on any of the best roads in the United States.

This result will be appreciated by the traveler who has once undergone the trials of a journey across the Isthmus during the days of the now obsolete mule and canoe. He will recall the long days and nights upon the Chagres river, and the hard ride over the rough road to Panama. He will think with a shudder how, swinging from the tall sides of the great steamer, tossing miles away in the swell of the open roadstead, which dashes its waves against the steep foundations of the rock-built fort of San Lorenzo, he timidly dropped into the slight canoe, which rose and fell like a bubble on the waves, and was finally cast ashore in the surf at the hazard of his life. He will recollect how, alternately chilled in the cold sea-waves, and broiled in the hot sun, he shuddered with a dread presentiment of Chagres' fever, as he went up the hot beach, and thence into the inhospitable pine-board settlement of Chagres. He will recollect how he shrunk from the gaunt spectres of Yankees who haunted the place, and who only reminded him of their humanity by their eager demands for his dollars. He will recollect the struggle with his thronging fellow-travelers for the scant boats; and if he had the good luck to secure a foot-rest in a crowded canoe, he will not forget how eagerly he sprung from the shore infected

CROSSING THE ISTHMUS IN THE OLDEN TIME.

with pestilence and vice. He will recollect the three days and nights of his wearisome ascent of the ever-bending river, the never-ceasing monotonous cries of the Negro boatmen, as they toiled along the banks, tugging at the overhanging foliage, startling the chattering monkeys, putting to flight the noisy parrots, and disturbing the sleepy alligators, which slided their huge, black, slimy bodies from the mud-reefs into the water. With the tedious monotony of his slow progress by day, and no rest at night, in his contracted canoe, shared with coarse adventurers, and no relief in the exorbitantly-paid entertainment at the hovels which stretched their mud-floors, and dispensed their stringy pork, muddy coffee, and wretched brandy by the wayside, for the refreshment of the traveler, he will recollect how spiritedly he took to mule at Cruces, and sped joyfully on until, soon jaded by the hard ride, he at last reached Panama, fatigued and dispirited, where, perhaps, if with powers of endurance equal to every trial, he slept, or if not, tossed restlessly about on his hard cot in the early agonies of fever. The old traveler will recollect all this, and rejoice in the comforts of the Panama Railroad.

Four days and nights was the usual duration of the journey from Chagres to Panama, and two days and nights from Panama to Chagres. The fatigue, the long exposure in an unhealthy climate, the deprivation of all comforts of eating, drinking, and sleeping, and the close jostling with a miscellaneous crowd of reckless adventurers, made the transit of the Isthmus impossible to travelers without a powerful stimulus, like that of the Californian gold excitement.

It was some time after the Railroad Company "broke ground" in December, 1850, that the old route to Panama was diverted from Chagres to Aspinwall. In July, 1852, only 23¼ miles of the railroad, from Aspinwall to Barbacoas, was ready for travel; and passengers thence went by the river Chagres to Gorgona or Cruces, and took to mule by the old road to Panama. In December, 1854, Culebra or the Summit, was the terminus; and not until January 27th, 1855, had a locomotive passed over the whole road of forty-nine miles, from ocean to ocean. Nearly five years were thus consumed before the entire track was practically fit for travel.

During my visit to the Isthmus, in the months of February and March, four sets of passengers to and from California, averaging about three hundred each, made the transit in the average time of four and a half hours, and on neither occasion was there aught to interfere with the personal enjoyment and safety of the traveler. During the intervals, however, although the train ran daily, there was an occasional detention. The yielding of the large embankment at the Summit, washed down by a heavy and unseasonable shower—for even the dry season has its rains not infrequently—detained the train all night, very *mal apropos*, and much to the discomfort of a pleasure party on their return from Aspinwall.

I was a sufferer on two occasions from the engine having run off the track. Once, at Aspinwall, where, being hurried through an early dinner by the impatient whistle of the engine, I seized my carpet-bag, and hastened away in the hot noonday sun, and found the locomotive, which had been just before so proudly snorting and so gayly showing its paces past the windows of the Mess House, silent and prostrate by the side of the track. My early dinner might have been prolonged into a late supper, in spite of the premature whistle of the engine; for the sun had nearly touched the green heights of the bay, and the tall masts of the shipping, and the cocoa-nut palms were throwing their long shadows upon the glistening white pier as the train started, and the deep darkness of a night in the forest had walled us in long before our arrival at Panama. On the second occasion, our party was on its return from the Railroad glorification on the Pacific, and had reached Obispo, some fifteen miles, when the engine again ran off the track, and forced us to spend the night in that delectable neighborhood, as will appear in the course of the narrative. These untoward circumstances arose from the incomplete construction of the road. The embankments not being thrown back to a sufficient distance, or properly secured, occasional slides of earth were unavoidable, and there not being the necessary switches or turn-tables, and the engine being driven in consequence backward upon a portion of the route, the running off the track was, of course, a not infrequent result.

The railroad then—though the great result of a direct communication between the Atlantic and Pacific has been effected—is still incomplete. Many miles of it are yet supported upon trestle-work—wooden props—which often lift the trains scores of feet in the air, whence the traveler, clutching fast to his seat, looks down upon deep gorges of rough, precipitous rock, and angry, swollen streams, with an alarm which is only relieved by his passage to the solid security of *terra firma*. There are also portions of the road where the train seems to feel its way with unusual caution, and jolts along with an irregularity of movement which is sure to excite the curiosity of the inquisitive, if not the fears of the anxious traveler. The knowing ones, if they are communicative and have no fear of Wall Street, will tell you that these are the *soft* parts of the road. And if you push your inquiries, you will learn that this *softness* is in consequence of the yielding soil, which has no more tenacity than softsoap, or the result of the decay of the sleepers, or cross-ties of native wood, which are crumbling into dust from the ceaseless borings of that busy little insect, the comihen, or rotting away in the quick decay of the hot, moist climate. The traveler, as he looks upon the pine buildings of the stations, and the wooden water-tanks, is surprised at the black stains of decay, the marks of ruin, and the rank growth which covers them, and hardly believes he is upon a new road just opened to travel, until he discovers that days quicken life and hasten death, in that region of rapid change, with greater speed than years in his own land of slow development. Time is no laggard in the tropics; and Life and Death follow his flying steps in quick succession. You may see by the roadside the giant trees, felled but a few months, already wrapt about with green shrouds of verdure, jeweled with sparkling flowrets, which a generous, reverential nature has thrown around the unsightly decay of these patriarchs of the forest. Again, wherever man's intrusive hand has bared the rock-ribbed mountain, or uncovered the fair bosom of the earth, a kind nature has thrown her flowing mantle of verdant growth.*

The deficiencies of the road are being promptly met by the inexhaustible energies of the chief engineer, and thousands of laborers are busy ballasting and filling in the trestle-work. Great piles of *lignum vitæ*, or *guaiacum* ties, brought from the forests of Carthagena, are heaped up by the roadside at Aspinwall, and will be substituted for the decayed ones of native wood. It is however believed, that even the toughness of the *lignum vitæ* will soon yield to the rapid decomposition of the climate of the Isthmus. In fact, there are some which have been tried not many months, which, according to one of the employés of the road,

* Such is the rapid growth of the vegetation, that there are parts of the road which require to be cleared twice a year; and there is little doubt that, if the road were left to itself for a single twelvemonth, it would not be discoverable by a solitary trace.

already show signs of decay. Stone masonry will be found necessary to give the road the permanency of a lasting institution. Iron bridges, which, the chief engineer authoritatively states, have been already "adopted," will be substituted for all the wooden structures. "Adopted"—the word Colonel Totten ingeniously, if not ingenuously, uses*—refers, however, it is supposed, to the operations at the railway-office in Broadway, for that gentleman pointed out an iron bridge of some half-dozen feet in length, as the only one "adopted" on the route, on the 2d March, 1855, out of some one hundred and thirty to be necessarily "adopted" in the future. The bridges vary from six feet to six hundred, and cross two large rivers, the Chagres and Gatun, and endless streams and gullies.

It will also be necessary to build the stations and tanks of brick, stone, iron, or of some more enduring material than wood, as they are rapidly falling into ruin, and look more like the antiquated remnants of the past, than the fresh structures of the enterprise of to-day. When these contemplated and necessary repairs and changes shall have been effected, the Panama Railroad will be a permanent monument of American skill and enterprise.

* New York Tribune, March 13.

The construction of the road was undertaken upon too narrow a basis, as to expenditure of money and labor. Stimulated by the hope of immediate gain, from the gold discovery, which was attracting the world to California, and flooding the Isthmus with an emigration which poured in torrents from the Atlantic to the Pacific, the commercial originators of the enterprise thought only of the tribute they might extort from the hurrying crowds of eager adventurers, or the gold they might glean from the rich harvest of the diggings of the Sacramento. The great object was to secure an immediate benefit from what was believed to be a temporary occasion. The practicability of a road was soon proved by the surveys of competent engineers, and estimates made of the cost. The former pleased Wall Street, for it showed the speculation feasible; the latter were received with dissatisfaction, for they threw doubt upon its paying. Accordingly, engineer after engineer was dismissed, until one was found whose arithmetic accorded with the close calculations of avaricious trade. A man of science, and great practical experience, had the candor to estimate the cost of the road at seven millions, and was, of course, pooh-poohed at the time, but would probably now be honored as a true prophet, as the result has justified the correctness of his calculations.

John L. Stephens, the traveler, however, must be excepted from those who, purely with mercenary motives, early engaged in the Panama Railroad enterprise. The grandeur of the union of the two oceans, the opening of a high road to the intercourse of all the world, the binding together of distant nations, and the consequent progress of civilization, warmed his imagination, and yielding up home, its comforts and its literary ease, in which he so much delighted, and sacrificing health and life in his devotion to the cause, he looked beyond the mere temptation of present gain, to the brighter prospect of furthering the interests of humanity.

With a parsimony which has turned out not to be by any means the best economy, the railroad was commenced as a temporary expedient, and constructed as hastily and cheaply as possible, that it might receive its share of the golden shower which was just then fertilizing American enterprise. Both the labor and expense exceeded the hopeful expectations of trade, and it was soon found that the supposed cost of three millions and a half would be doubled, and that the difficulties were so great that the hundreds of laborers would have to be increased to thousands, and the era for the consummation of the great undertaking postponed from 1853 to 1855. A more liberal and comprehensive view of the necessities of the enterprise would have provided, from the commencement, against the present unavoidable reconstruction, the substitution of iron bridges and more enduring ties, the building of new dépôts and stations, and the long postponement of the completion of the road.

However incomplete the present result, the difficulties in its accomplishment have been great, and the enterprise with which they have been overcome in the highest degree creditable. The Isthmus did not supply a single resource necessary for the undertaking. Not only the capital, skill, and enterprise, but the labor, the material, the wood and iron, the daily food, the clothing, the roof to cover, and the instrument to work with, came from abroad. The United States supplied the enterprising capitalists, the men of science, the engineers, the practical business managers, the superior workmen, the masons, carpenters, and forgers of iron. Distant parts of the world supplied the laborers. From Ireland came crowds of her laborious peasantry. The Negroes, stimulated to unusual energy by the prospect of reward, thronged in from Jamaica. The surplus populations of India and China contributed their share. The mixed races of the province of Carthagena, the Indian, Spaniard, and African completed this representation of all nations, in which the Caucasian, Mongolian, and African, the Anglo-American, European, Negro, American-Indian, and Asiatic, with all their diverse temperaments, habits, and religious faiths, mingled together appropriately to join in a work by which the ends of the earth were to be brought together for the common interests of the whole world.

Most of the material used for the construction of the road was brought from vast distances. Although the country abounded in forests, it was found necessary, from the expense of labor and the want of routes of communication, to send the timber for the most part from the United States; and not only were the rails, to a considerable extent, laid on American pine, but the bridges, and the houses and workshops of the various settlements were of the same wood, all fashioned in Maine and Georgia. The metal-work, the rails, the locomotives, and the tools were brought either from England or the United States. The daily food of the laborer even, came from a New York market.

Fleets of vessels from all parts of the world

sailed into the harbor of Aspinwall. Ships arrived from Cork crowded with Irish emigrants. From Bombay and Hong Kong came the East Indiamen thronged with Coolies and Chinamen. From the United States, steamer after steamer brought hundreds of skillful workmen. From Jamaica the little white schooners, loaded with Negroes, came in quick succession. The smart American coasters briskly arrived with their supplies of timber and provisions from the Atlantic coast; and great lumbering hulks floated into port, with their heavy freight of iron and coal from the mines of Great Britain. The whole world was put under tribute for the great enterprise.

To the difficulties which naturally ensued from undertaking an enterprise the resources of which had to be gathered from the remote ends of the world, were added the natural obstacles of the country. Forests, so closely interwoven with thick growth that they were impenetrable to light, which had darkened the country in perpetual night for ages, had to be cleared. Walls of jungle had to be struck down, and treacherous swamps, in which man had never before ventured, had to be made firm as a foundation of rock. Here was a gigantic work sufficient to task all the energies of enterprise and the full strength of labor. When to this was added a climate which disposes, from its prostrating heat, to indolence, and an atmosphere the malignant breathing of which is poison, the result which has been accomplished seems almost superhuman.

The unhealthiness of the climate has been one of the most serious obstacles against which the enterprise has struggled. I need not dwell upon the causes which produce those diseases which are endemic on the Isthmus. The alternation of the wet and dry season, a perpetual summer-heat, and the decomposition of the profuse tropical vegetation, must of course generate an intense miasmatic poison, and I was not surprised when the oldest and most experienced of the physicians employed on the railroad declared to me that no one, of whatever race or country, who becomes a resident of the Isthmus, escapes disease.

I am indebted to the same gentleman just mentioned, for some interesting facts. From him I learned that those who were exposed to the miasmatic poison of the country were generally taken ill in four or five weeks, although sometimes, but rarely, not for four or five months after exposure. That the first attack was generally severe; and took the form of yellow, bilious remittent, or malignant intermittent fever. That although none were exempt, the miasmatic poison affected the various races with different degrees of rapidity. That the African resisted the longest, next the Cooly, then the European, and last in order the Chinese, who gave in at once. The rate of mortality, I was informed, was, for the natives of all races, one in fifty, the Coolies, one in forty, the Negroes (foreign), one in forty, the Europeans, one in thirty, and the Chinese, one in ten. Those who recover from the immediate effects of the first attack are liable to an habitual fever and ague. The system never habituates itself to the miasmatic poison, and complete recovery from fever, during a residence on the Isthmus, is impossible. The sufferer may arise from his bed of sickness, but totters up and stalks about a mere ghost of his former self. It is thus that I never met with a wholesome-looking person among all those engaged upon the railroad. There was not one whose constitution had not been sapped by disease, and all, without exception, are in the almost daily habit of taking medicine to drive away the ever-recurring fever and ague.* I accosted,

* The Railroad Company are so far conscious of the debility engendered by a residence on the Isthmus, that they

on one occasion, a gang of six Negro laborers from Jamaica—the whole number engaged in working a hand-car—and each one told me he had had fever, although neither of them had been in the country over six months. The universal answer, to my universal question, "How do you like the country?" was, "Not at all, because of the fever."

My medical friend added his to the universal testimony in favor of quinine, which he declared to be the most effective antidote to the miasmatic poison. This drug he is in the habit of prescribing in moderate doses, and at once, without any preparatory treatment of the patient. In common with all, the doctor advocated temperate habits, and condemned the use of strong stimulants in health and disease; although the moderate use of claret wine, or the light, bitter ale was gently recommended; perhaps from a polite concession to the tastes of his guest, who discussed these interesting subjects with him, over a creaming bottle of Alsop's best East India beer, which I always relished,

refuse to employ those laborers who, having gone to a healthier climate to recruit, return to seek employment. It is found that such are unprofitable servants, and yield at once to the enervating and sickening climate. The enterprise requires all the vigor of unweakened sinews, and of pure, wholesome blood.

drank plentifully of during my stay on the Isthmus, and never suffered from.

My note book contains the following, with which I will close my tedious professional talk: "Accidents rare on the road; recovery difficult from prostration; bones unite with difficulty, in consequence of complication from fever; operations upon natives and Africans tolerably successful; scorpion bites not serious; tarantula bites occasionally followed by erysipelatous inflammation; bilious colics and constipation abound; diseases of the eye are cured with great rapidity; ulcerations of the cornea heal in two weeks without cicatrix."

A terrible fatality attended the efforts of the Railroad Company to avail themselves of the assistance of the Chinese laborers. A ship arrived, and landed on the Isthmus some eight hundred, after a fair voyage from Hong Kong, where these poor devils of the flowery kingdom had unwittingly sold themselves to the service of the railroad, perfectly ignorant of the country whither they were going, and of the trials which awaited them. The voyage was tolerably prosperous, and the Chinese bore its fatigues and sufferings with great patience, cheered by the prospects of reaching the foreign land, whither they had been tempted by the glowing descriptions of those traffickers in human life, who had so liberally promised them wealth and happiness. Sixteen died on the passage, and were thrown into the sea. No sooner had the eight hundred survivors landed, than thirty-two of the number were struck down prostrate by sickness; and in less than a week afterward, eighty more laid by their side. The interpreters who accompanied them, attributed this rapid prostration to the want of their habitual opium. This drug was then distributed among them, and with the good effect of so far stimulating their energies, that two-thirds of the sick arose again from their beds, and began to labor. A Maine opium law, however, was soon promulgated on the score of the immorality of administering to so pernicious a habit, and without regard, it is hoped, to the expense; which, however, was no inconsiderable item, since the daily quota of each Chinese amounted to fifteen grains, at the cost of at least fifteen cents. Whether it was owing to the deprivation of their habitual stimulus, or the malignant effects of the climate, or home-sickness, or disappointment, in a few weeks there was hardly one out of the eight hundred Chinese who was not prostrate and unfit to labor. The poor sufferers let the pick and the shovel fall from their hands, and yielded themselves up to the agony of despair. They now gladly welcomed death, and impatiently awaited their turn in the ranks which were falling before the pestilence. The havoc of disease went on, and would have done its work in time; but as it was sometimes merciful, and spared a life, and was deliberate though deadly, the despairing Chinese could wait no longer: he hastily seized the hand of death, and voluntarily sought destruction in its grasp. Hundreds destroyed themselves, and showed, in their various modes of suicide, the characteristic Chinese ingenuity. Some deliberately lighted their pipes, and sat themselves down upon the shore of the sea, and awaited the rising of the tide—grimly resolved to die—and sat and sat, silent and unmoved as a storm-beaten rock, as wave arose above wave, until they sank into the depths of eternity. Some bargained with their companions for death—giving their all to the friendly hand which, with a kindly touch of the trigger, would scatter their brains, and hasten their doom. Some hung themselves to the tall trees by their hair, and some twisted their queues about their necks, with a deliberate coil after coil, until their faces blackened, their eye-balls started out, their tongues protruded, and death relieved their agony. Some cut ugly, crutch-shaped sticks, sharpened the ends to a point, and thrust their necks upon them until they were pierced through and through, and thus mangled, yielded up life in a torrent of blood. Some took great stones into their hands, and leaped into the depths of the nearest river, and clung, with resolute hold, to the weight which sunk them, gurgling in the agonies of drowning, to the bottom, until death loosened their grasp, and floated them to the surface, lifeless bodies. Some starved themselves to death—refusing either to eat or drink. Some impaled themselves upon their instruments of labor—and thus, in a few weeks after their arrival, there were but scarce two hundred Chinese left of the whole number. This miserable remnant of poor, heart-sick exiles, prostrate from the effects of the climate, and bent on death, being useless for labor, were sent to Jamaica, where they have, ever since, lingered out a miserable beggar's life.

The Railroad Company was hardly more fortunate with another importation of live freight. A cargo of Irish laborers from Cork reached Aspinwall, and so rapidly did they yield to the malignant effects of the climate, that not a good day's labor was obtained from a single one; and so great was the mortality, that it was found necessary to ship the survivors to New York, where most died from the fever of the Isthmus which was fermenting in their blood. The laborers now employed, to the number of three thousand, on the road are of the mixed native races, chiefly from the province of Cathagena, Negroes from Jamaica, and Coolies from the East Indies.

The police of the road is not among the least arduous and expensive of the duties of the Company. The impotent government of New Granada, finding itself too weak to exert the necessary authority to control the large body of men employed as laborers on the road —many of whom are of a class requiring the strictest *surveillance*—has delegated full powers to the Company. Accordingly the Railroad officials have taken into their hands the police of the Isthmus, and exercise it with no weak sway. An armed guard, to the number of forty, was enrolled, and placed under the command of Ran Runnels, the famous Texian Ranger, of whom many deeds of daring and of fierce determination are recorded, by which he has made himself a terror to evil-doers. The casual observer would not remark any thing very formidable in the delicate organization of the bold Ran. He is of short stature, and of a slight built frame. His hand is small, and looks better suited for a lady's kid glove than to handle bowie-knife or revolver. His boyish, well-combed head, and delicate features, indicate little of the daring spirit of the man; but there is a close, resolute, pressure of the thin lips, a commanding glance of the eye, a sinewy wiryness of the limbs, and an activity of movement, which are in character with his bold determination and lively energies. His guard of forty are not very impressive in appearance. A military martinet might object to such a loose assortment of bravadoes, of all colors, heights, and varieties of dress. Negroes, Mulattoes, and white men mingle indiscriminately in the ranks, who, however effective in service, would not make a much fairer show on parade than Falstaff's Ragged Regiment. A bare-footed, coatless, harum-scarum-looking set they are, and might easier pass for the forty thieves, than that

RAN RUNNELS.

number of honest guards. With Ran Runnels, however, at their head they have cleared the Isthmus of robbers, and kept the thousands of unruly laborers in wholesome subjection. The Railroad Company, appreciating their services, have bestowed the liberal largess of from two to four thousand dollars a month upon Ran and his Ragged Regiment.

Whipping, imprisonment, and shooting down, in an emergency, have been liberally inflicted in the exercise of the powers delegated by the government of New Granada to the Company, which has the power of life and death on the Isthmus without appeal.

In spite of all the difficulties enumerated, the Panama Railroad is now an accomplished fact, and the traveler can pass from ocean to ocean with facility and comfort; and when the details of construction and reconstruction, now in progress, shall have been completed, the road will undoubtedly be as secure and permanent as the best in the world. Fully to realize the advantages of the road, however, it will be necessary to pass the traveler to and from California, from steamer to steamer, immediately on his arrival. It is especially to be wished, on the score of humanity, apart from considerations of facilitating commercial intercourse, that no one should be unnecessarily delayed a single hour in that fatal town of Aspinwall, or in the unhealthy city of Panama. This desirable object can be readily attained by always having a steamer in reserve at either terminus; and such is, it is believed, the intention of the various steamboat proprietaries. Notwithstanding the unquestionably superior comforts of the Isthmus route to California, it has not yet monopolized the passenger traffic, for the simple reason that hitherto the journey, by the way of Nicaragua, has always been accomplished in a day or two less time. With swift boats, however, on the Atlantic and Pacific, and no detention on the Isthmus, the route by Panama and Aspinwall can be made the briefer in time, as it is undoubtedly the more comfortable and convenient.

The cost of the railroad has much exceeded the original expectations of the Company. A competent writer in the *New York Tribune*, of the date of March 13, 1855, estimates it at seven millions. Colonel Totten, the engineer, declares, however, that six millions is the extent of the cost; but this sum does not probably include the expense of the reconstruction of parts of the road, the substitution of iron bridges, which have been "adopted," the laying down of *lignum vitæ* ties, and other changes acknowledged to be necessary. The same writer whom I have quoted estimates the aggregate receipts at $730,000, while Colonel Totten, the engineer, declares that this sum is much below the actual amount; and it has been stated that $120,000 was received from the traffic of the single month of March.

The want of a harbor at Panama is an insuperable obstacle to the carrying of heavy freight, without a very important and expensive addition to the construction of the road. At present the terminus at the Pacific Ocean is outside the gates of the city of Panama, and all freight as well as passengers must be conveyed a distance of at least two miles to ship—the harbor not admitting sea-vessels of any considerable draft nearer to the shore. The expense of lighterage and the necessary damage which attends it, are such as to render such a mode of conveyance of freight impracticable. The Railroad Company are perfectly aware of the incompleteness of their work, and, having purchased three islands in the bay, propose to establish a harbor at one of them, and connect the whole to the mainland by means of a pier, in order that the Railroad may terminate at the sides of the ship. Another plan—that of building a dock like those of Liverpool—has been proposed. Either will be a great undertaking, worthy of the enterprise which has already effected so much, and one or the other will be absolutely necessary fully to accomplish the great purpose of the Railroad, that of revolutionizing the course of trade of the world, by diverting it from the old channel of Cape Horn. The millions which may be required to carry out this design will not be held back by those who have already poured out with no grudging hand their generous largesses for the benefit of commercial enterprise. When this consummation of the noble design shall be effected, and the channel of trade changed, the Panama Railroad will become, in the language of the enthusiastic Darien projector Patterson, the "Door of the Seas, and the Key of the Universe." Then will the commercial enterprise and scientific skill which have begun this wonder of the age be rewarded with something more substantial than glory—a remunerative balance sheet to their credit account.

NOTE.

M. Emile Chevalier, in an article on the Panama Railroad in the *Revue des Deux Mondes* of June 1, 1850, makes the following estimate of the cost and revenue of the road:

Cost	$4,900,000
Gross receipts	860,000
Annual expense	344,000
Net revenue	516,000

being about ten per cent. upon the sum supposed to be expended. In this estimate, however, the cost is underrated. Colonel Totten, the chief engineer, acknowledges it to have been six millions on the 12th March, which is probably two millions less than the actual sum which has been, or will be, expended. M. Chevalier, moreover, exaggerates the number of passengers, which he puts down at 30,000—ten thousand beyond the real amount—annually, and the quantity of specie transported, which he estimates at 100,000,000—four times the average sum.

The estimate of a writer in the *New York Tribune*, of the date of March 13, is as follows:

"At present, the only revenue is from passengers, the mails, specie, and express parcels, the aggregate amount of which is not above $730,000. If the road should enjoy the monopoly of California travel, this may be increased two or three hundred thousand dollars, provided the number of passengers to and from California should not diminish, whereas it is diminishing year by year. Suppose the possible revenue to be one million, leaving out of consideration all heavy freight-carrying, which we consider out of the question in the present state of the road, the expenses can never be much less than fifty per cent. of the gross receipts. At this moment there are 3,000 laborers employed, at eighty cents a day for work, and thirty cents for support, a large number of mechanics who receive from two to three dollars daily, and thirty officials, paid about $100,000, making a total of more than a million of dollars. This array of workmen and laborers will be required for a long time yet, and we question whether more than a half of them can ever be dispensed with. There is a great deal still to be done on the road, in the way of embankment, substitution of new ties, iron for wooden bridges, etc. Moreover, such is the nature of the climate, the destructive character of the atmosphere and the insects, and the rapid growth of vegetation, that there will always be work for an army of laborers. Five hundred thousand dollars a year I believe to be a small estimate of the annual expenses of the road, and one million a large estimate of the revenue. We have left half a million for net income to pay the interest upon a capital of seven millions."

The following statement, by a merchant of Panama, is valuable, and shows the impracticability of the railroad route for the conveyance of freight at the present rate of charge:

"Previous to the discovery of gold in California, the charge for transporting merchandise across the Isthmus from *Cruces* or *Gorgona*, villages on the banks of the river Chagres, was about 1½ cent per pound. After the emigration to California commenced the price rose to from 20 to 40 cents per pound, and decreased as the number of mules increased, to from 15 to 18 cents per pound, until the railroad was opened to the Summit, alias Culebra, when it decreased to from 9 to 7 cents. The present rates of freight by the railroad, the merchants of the South Pacific will not pay while they can obtain freight round the Horn from Europe, at from $15 to $18 per tun, except it be for costly goods such as silks, fine muslins, jewelry, &c. The freight on merchandise by the steamers from Southampton, is £6 ($30) per tun, measurement, to Colon; and to Guayaquil from Panama, by steamer, $22 per tun, measurement; to Payta from Panama, by steamer, $15 per tun, measurement; to Callao from Panama, by steamer, $18 per tun, measurement; to Valparaiso from Panama, by steamer, $25 per tun, measurement; to San Francisco, $80 for expresses, and $100 for other merchandise, per tun, measurement. The specie consisting generally of coined silver, and silver in bars, brought by the English steamers, from the South Pacific coast, is not conveyed across the Isthmus by the railroad, owing to the charge by this conveyance being ½ per cent, while it can be sent from Panama on mules to Cruces or Gorgona, and from thence down the river in barges or canoes, to Chagres for less than ¼ per cent."

The following extract from the terms of contract with the Government of New Granada will show to what extent the large capital, say eight millions, is endangered, apart from insufficient revenue, as an investment in the Panama road:

"At the expiration of twenty years, counted from the day on which the railroad shall have been completed and opened to public use, the government may redeem the privilege for the benefit of New Granada, by the sum of five millions of dollars, to be paid as the whole amount of the indemnification. If the privilege should not be redeemed at that date, it shall continue in force ten years longer in favor of the Panama Railroad Company, and at the end of that time the government may redeem it by paying four millions of dollars; if it be not redeemed at the end of this latter period, it shall continue in force ten years still longer, at the end of which the government may redeem it by paying two millions of dollars. In order that the government may avail itself of the right thus reserved to it of redeeming the privilege, it shall notify the Panama Railroad Company of its intention to redeem the privilege, during the year preceding the day of the expiration of either of the three periods above expressed."

CHAPTER V.

WALK ABOUT PANAMA.

OUR party, overflowing with holiday spirit, in full possession of the bare rooms, wide halls, and spreading balconies of the Aspinwall House, created a new soul within the ribs of the old hotel, which was fast dying of inanition, and cheered the desponding landlord with a hope of paying his quarter's rent. The Jamaica Negro, Thomas, the factotum of the establishment, grinned a hearty welcome as he clutched our carpet-bags with all the hunger of a starved porter; he sprang up the great stone steps, shuffled along the corridors, and ushered us with great glee into the immense rooms, where the uncarpeted cedar-floors, the thick, whitewashed walls, the enormous windows without a pane of glass or a casement, and closed in with large, green-painted, spreading shutters, like barn doors, did not present any very encouraging prospect of bedchamber-comfort; the skeleton cots, however, from which their living souls had long since departed, ranged along the wall by the half-dozen together, gave security of no want of companionship. Warmth of hospitality, however, can be dispensed with in the torrid zone; and we found naked, thick walls, bare cedar-floors, perpetually open windows, and meagre cots, without a mattress below or a coverlet above, more favorable to repose than all the appointments of a more luxurious upholstery.

Most of our company had but two days to spend at Panama, and much of that time had been appropriated in advance to the celebration as laid down in the programme. There was the excursion to Taboga to be undergone; the lunch of the English Steam Company to be eaten; and, as if a feast spread by the substantial hospitality of John Bull were not quite enough for at least twenty-four hours, there was to be digested, on the same day, the prodigious banquet of the Railroad Company, with its long speeches, which, although so well masticated, were rather tough morsels to swallow.

Our company, as they were guests, felt it to be their first duty to respond to the hospitality of their entertainers; and accordingly, having refreshed themselves with iced brandy-and-water, Champagne cock-tails, which had now become habitual in spite of our better principles, and with oranges, pines, bananas, papaws, mangoes, and other luscious fruit to satiety, they sallied out into the city, and went laboriously to work in the hot sun, to do their utmost in sight-seeing. Separating into various groups, Panama was very effectually investigated by us Yankee visitors. Now some went straggling along the narrow streets, pricing Panama hats in the shops, and ogling the dark señoritas, who lounged in loose costume in the wooden balconies, which, ranging one above the other in the houses, threw their shadows across the road. Some strolled with profane steps, heathen Protestants as they were, through the arched entrances of the old churches, decrepit with ruin, mouldy with decay, and almost hid in the green growth which sprung luxuriantly from every gaping crevice, and pushed their way into the very precincts of the sanctuary, where they cast irreverent eyes upon painted-faced, spangled-robed virgins, and honored saints, in suits of yellow turned up with blue which were rather the worse for wear. The young girl, prostrate upon the stone pavement, pouring out her soul in prayer, and the tottering old man bent in trembling worship at the feet of those gaudy images, made up of wood, tarnished gilt, yellow ochre, and rags, should have awed the profane visitors; but they turned upon their heels from the true devotion which these worshipers were wringing from their hearts, and went about scoffing at all they saw, sneering at the frouzy padres, sniffing at the tallow candles, peering into the rotting confessional-boxes, and thrusting their profane fingers into the latticed earlets, through which so many anxious hearts had palpitated the inmost secrets of their lives into the eager ears of their father-confessors.

Out of church our unbelieving countrymen pass, perhaps, into the neighboring drinking-saloon, where their patriotism is no doubt warmed by the sight of a spruce bar-keeper in linen jacket from their own native land, compounding a draught for a brother Yankee, whose bilious eyes, yellow face, and shaky hand, tell of the effects of the climate, and oft-repeated calls for bitters. Two meagre youths of native blood are busy at the billiard-table. Some half-dozen Spaniards and Frenchmen are playing dominoes under the porch, and refreshing themselves with beer and absynthe. The American is at home here, for he hears his own language expressed with the usual idiomatic elegance prevailing in such refined society; sees in the range of crystal bottles, brilliantly set off with gilded labels, and bright with variously-colored liquids, familiar objects; observes such swaggering manners as he need not travel far from home to witness; sniffs up an atmosphere, which has a very distinct flavor of his own land, reeking as it is with brandy and redolent of cigars, and as he turns into the fresh air, is not surprised to see by the staring sign that he has just taken his sherry-cobbler in the United States, Washington, or St. Charles saloon, as it may be.

Along the narrow street some of us go, out into the Plaza, bare and desert-like, and see here and there a shackled mule cropping the parched grass, a group of naked Negro children playing upon the steps of the great ruined church, and a line of galley slaves clanking their manacles, as with sodden looks and lingering steps they are driven by the armed Mulatto guard to the prison hard by, through the iron bars of which, and from the darkness within, start out the glaring eye-balls of an ugly-looking Negro fellow, who, we congratulate ourselves, is well secured. From the Plaza, down a street bounded on each side by heavy stone houses, we can see, through the arched gate of the old wall which surrounds the city, the waters of the bay glistening in the sun; so we stroll in that direction, passing a freshly whitewashed building, from which droops in the hot, breathless noonday, the stars and stripes, while beneath their folds brightens the glowing face of a very hot American Consul, who is doing his best to ventilate himself in the balcony above us, and by whom we are recognized, and accordingly invited to the brandy-and-water hospitalities of the Consulate, which, flow in never-ceasing streams. Opposite the stars and stripes is the office of the *Panama Star*, where the newspaper reporters of our party have already announced their arrival, and been duly honored with a record of their names in the *Court Gazette.* Going down the street just by the wall gate, we come to a heavy prison-like building, from the barred windows of which, overlooking the ruined wall, must be a fine view of the bay, and we do not doubt those poor nuns said to be incarcerated there — for the building is a convent — enjoy it, if that much of the outer world is spared them. With a whirl of the turning box, a knock at the convent gate, and a fierce rebuke for our heretical impertinence from a savage, grinning Negress, who was the she-dragon that guarded the sweet love-apples closely stowed away—the duenna who held watch over the, of course, lovely señoritas within—we turn away from the frousiness of that remnant of decayed antiquity to air ourselves in the fresh breeze on the Rampart.

The Rampart is the choice promenade of the city. Its ruined walls, tottering turrets with their loopholes jagged and torn by the tooth of time, its dismantled guns, elaborately wrought of brass and richly embossed, brought, hun dreds of years ago, from the great foundries of Barcelona, to defend the wealth of Panama from the buccaneers of old, and the jealous enemies of Spain in its days of grandeur and galleons, give a melancholy aspect of decay. But the foundations, laid two centuries since, strong upon the rocky reef, yet uphold the wide esplanade, scores of feet high, solid and secure from the perpetual swell of the ocean, which rolls in here its great waves, and dashes them against the base, until they are driven back high in the air in cataracts of foam. The Rampart stands upon the point projecting seaward of the tongue of land upon which Panama is built. Before us, looking southward, are groups of green islands, which diversify the wide expanse of the bay. There are Taboga and Taboguilla in the distance—ten miles away —with fleets of shipping safely anchored in their harbors. Closer, within two miles or so, are

THE RAMPART OF PANAMA.

the islands of Flamenco, Perico, and Llenao, upon the sides of which the cocoa-nut palms can be seen rising from the white surf of the shore. From these green islands, starting out of the sea, in perpetual verdure from base to summit, upon the hills and valleys of which the capricious sky is throwing bright glances and deep shadows in quick alternation, the eye passes beyond to those distant groups, half hid in a purple light, and thence to the dark horizon, beyond which extends the great ocean.

On the right and left of the observer, as he still faces the south, the bay bends into irregular inlets, here, washing a stretch of white beach glistening in the sun, and there, bathing the base of mountains of verdure, which, rising from the shore, extend their irregular heights far inland. Panama stretches back of the Rampart, and shows its ruined churches, and its dark, mouldy houses, irregularly grouped about the shore on either side, until it is lost in the thick shade of the hills of forest which connect the tongue of land, upon which the city is built, with the main-land.

There is hardly a living soul to be met, in these dead times of Panama, upon the Rampart. A few months ago, it was alive with swaggering Californians, who were wont to turn up their noses at the defunct artillery, and show the vitality of their own ready shooters by firing off their six-barreled revolvers, to the imminent risk of the lives of all who were within pistol-shot. Now, beyond an occasional señorita, half-hid in her black vail, expectant of her lover; an Indian nurse, with a pale, sickly white child, gasping for a breath of wholesome air; a contemplative old Spaniard, smoking his cigar, and ventilating his Panama hat and linen jacket in the sea-breeze, or a curious stranger, there are no visitors to the Rampart. There is still a scant show of military possession in the neighborhood of the fortification; but we question whether among those Mulatto fellows, in bare feet, loose tow-cloth jackets and trowsers, and red flannel caps, who keep up a perpetual fire of cigars from the windows of the ruined barracks, down in the trench behind the Rampart there is a force or military skill enough to load one of the old cannon.

The various groups of our party, gathering from all parts of the city, meet together at dinner at Victor's. The Aspinwall House confined its hospitality at the rate of three dollars per cot to lounging by day and sleeping at night; our entertainers of the Railroad Company, therefore, had given their guests the free run of Monsieur Victor's kitchen. Accordingly we ate our breakfast eggs, and our dinner steaks, and drank our claret, and our *chasse café* at Victor's famous Restaurant. Monsieur Victor, *bon patriote* that he is, was true to the traditional forms of the glorious cuisine of his native land, but was sadly false to its substance. He indulged in all sorts of patriotic reminiscences of *la belle France* on his bill of fare, but his table proved him recreant to his country. The grand flourish of *fillets*, *blanquettes*, *entremets*, *legumes*, and *fines herbes*, which Monsieur Victor daily exposed to our view, written in the neatest of hands on the whitest of paper, were creditable evidences of the patriotic heart that still beats beneath Monsieur Victor's white waistcoat, but they did not satisfy the hungry stomachs which were collapsed beneath the waistcoats of his guests. His *fillets*, *blanquettes*, and *entremets*, were everlasting tough beef, and his *legumes* and *fines herbes* were perpetual garlic. Monsieur Victor's ponderous silver forks and spoons, and his tall castors of oil cruets were very imposing; but I would recommend Monsieur to sell out that *argenterie*, and invest the proceeds in a washerwoman. The necessary peck of dirt, carefully distributed in installments during a week at the least, would be probably more acceptable than crowding it all at once into the sugar-bowl; while a clean table-cloth occasionally, is politely suggested as an improvement of the filthy spread upon which Monsieur Victor daily displays his uninviting banquet.

The best things I could find to eat were the pigeons which abound on the Isthmus; and, when Monsieur Victor concentrated his energies on a *pigeon grillè*, I could forgive him for his fast-decaying reminiscences of the French cuisine, in the shape of his India-rubber *fillets*, and his *fricandeaus de veau* of tough rags. Fish, although abounding in the bay, I seldom could get, for the natives are too lazy to catch it or to bring it to market. Iguano steaks and monkey ragouts are pronounced excellent; but my stay being short on the Isthmus, I did not care to admit such foreigners to a naturalization in my native American stomach. Fruits of all kinds can be had at Panama, but never at a very moderate price, for here again the indolence of the natives interferes with an abundant supply. The oranges are excellent, so are the bananas, the papaws, the mangoes, the pines, the cheromoyas, and the thousand other luscious products. Yams and yucas abound, and are a fair substitute for the potato, which last does not grow on the Isthmus, but is supplied at a fair price from the coasts of Peru and Chili. The French wines are generally drank at Panama, and Monsieur Victor supplied us with some acrid specimens of St. Julien and Barsac. There are no native beverages but the chichas, fermented drinks made from the pine-apple, maize, and other native products. I attempted a calabash of chicha on one occasion, and although impressed with the advice of my friend, that "it was good for me," I could not get beyond the first glutinous, mussy taste, and accordingly remained uncognizant of the benefits of chicha.

At our dinner at Victor's, our party compared notes of their observations on the city. Old W——, of Connecticut, had been every where. He had visited the ruined monasteries and convents, and suggested that a few hundred shingles might stop up the gaps of time and keep the rain out; he had beheld with pious horror the naked piccaninies wallowing in the gutters, and advised, with Christian benevolence, a supply of shirts and wooden schoolhouses; he had strolled into the neighboring forest, and seemed to be of opinion that a clearing and well-cultivated farms would be an improvement. The fashionable B——, of New York, did not think the streets comparable to Broadway, and thought the women by no means genteel, as they walked the streets without hats, and wore their flounces at the top of the neck instead of at the bottom of their feet. One had his experiences to relate of the market, another of the burying-ground. The man of business concluded that Panama was decidedly dull, while the poet of the company declared

"A pleasing land of drowsy head it was."

From dinner I return to our hotel, which is but a step or so from Victor's, and mounting to the balcony, which overhangs the street, observe the passing life. The cavalcade of riders, mostly the foreign residents returning from their afternoon ride, come clattering down the paved road, with their ambling mules and brisk little white Peruvian stallions, richly caparisoned with silver-mounted bridles and gayly-adorned high-peaked Spanish saddles.

A spruce-looking padre passes, on his return from vespers, in long silk surplice, the gossamer skirts of which flowing in the breeze reveal a bright, pink satin lining, loose drawers of the finest linen, gathered at the knees with golden buckles, and black silk hose, terminating in a pair of the smallest, brightly-polished shoes, set off with buckles of pure gold. A cocked beaver hat, turned up with white silk, and adorned with fringe and tassels, and a gold-headed cane, complete the costume of the dandy priest. The shining olive face and glossy black hair of the "oily man of God," the gusto with which he puffs his cigar, and the gallant manner with which he accosts the pretty dark girls of his flock, show him to be no anchorite. In fact, there is no more gallant Don Juan in the parish; and, in spite of his celibacy, his children outnumber those of the patriarchs. As for the minor morals, he is a sad transgressor, if the scandal is to be believed that only last week he staked those golden buckles on a game at *monte*, and lost at a cock-fight his last fee for lifting a soul from purgatory.

PADRE.

Next comes a slouchy Negro woman, with her long hair streaming down her back, and her sleek, ebony body half out of her loose gown, which, in accordance with the usual fashion on the Isthmus, has its flounces at the top instead of the bottom. She carries her great Negro-baby, as naked as it was born, astraddle her hip, which seems to be dislocated for the express purpose. She, like all the world, is smoking the eternal cigar. Then follow a mother and child, gayly bedizened with all the finery of bright-ribboned Panama hats, loose calico dresses of brilliant pattern, bright-red satin slippers stuck upon the tips of thoroughly African feet, whence project backward, as the Irishman would say, unmistakable Negro heels. The child is a perfect miniature of her mother from hat to slipper, displays the same superfluity of black skin, wears the same gay calico with its reversed flounces, and rejoices in an equally gorgeous chain of golden eagles about her neck. The two seem impressed with the magnificence of their appearance, and walk with measured steps of conscious pride through the street.

WOMAN AND CHILD.

MOTHER AND CHILD.

There goes another characteristic denizen of the old town—the water-carrier—on his mule. He is just returning from outside the walls, where he has filled his kegs from the orange-shaded spring, and comes in, in the cool evening, to empty his moist kegs into the great, red, earthen, porous vessels of his customers, which may be seen under the shade of every balcony, exuding from their surface a perpetually cool moisture. Each keg seems to be germinating with growth, for a tuft of green leaves inserted into the holes at the top, serves to keep the water from being jolted out on the route.

WATER-CARRIER.

As the shades of evening gather, the city becomes quite animated. Groups of native and foreign dandies come out of their shops and counting-houses, in the dark recesses of which they have been hiding themselves during the day from the sun, and congregate at the corner, where they shine "all glossy gay" in black silk French sacks, Panama hats, white trowsers, and varnished boots, or seat themselves under the portico of the St. Charles saloon, opposite, in the enjoyment of cigars and sherry-cobblers, cooled with Boston ice. The Jamaica Negro women are sidling in and out among the groups, ringing loud with laughter, and offering, with pert banter, the fruits and cakes they carry poised upon their heads.

As the night advances, the streets become emptied, and are left to silence; and the moon, glowing in those tropical latitudes almost with the glare of a noonday sun, brightens up the houses opposite with a golden light, and throws the shadow of the balcony of the Aspinwall House upon the pavement, with the distinct outline of a drawing. Yet late in the night, the clattering of the billiard-balls, and the clinking of glasses in the bar-room below, are distinctly heard, which somewhat disturb the pleasant thoughts of Gil Blas and his romantic companions, the licentiates, caballeros, and señoritas of Madrid, Salamanca, and Toledo, suggested by the tingling of a guitar from beneath the balcony opposite. With a sleepy confusion of the old and the new, I turn into my cot, and sleep until morning.

Next morning we were all agog at an early hour for the trip to the island of Taboga, where the agent of the English Pacific Mail Steamship Company had invited us to a lunch. Accordingly we all gathered, dressed in our best suits of linen and drilling, the remnants of the last New York summer's wear, about Monsieur Victor's dirty spread, and having tried to eat his tough fillets, and his jumbled-up omelets which were bad, and succeeded in drinking his coffee, which, apart from the loads of dirt in the sugar, was good (*Mem.* They have the very best coffee in Panama, brought from Ponta Arenas on the Pacific, a hundred miles or so north of the bay, where a couple of ship's cargoes are annually raised, surpassing in aroma and richness of flavor the best Mocha), we strolled down the street, just as the black, vailed señoritas and the slouchy Negresses, in flaunting calicoes, were returning from matins, and soon reached the spacious, thick-walled stone dwelling and offices of the agent of the United States Mail Pacific Steamship Company. Here there was a half hour's detention, in the course of which we made the acquaintance of the pale-faced lady of the mansion, a sick baby, an irritable monkey, which, after various attempts in vain to conciliate with the better-half of a mango, we found it advisable to leave to the full run of its chain along the balcony, a chattering parrot, which swung from the heavy rafters above and spoke Spanish with a volubility which put Captain S——, who prided himself upon his Castilian, to the blush, and of an ant-eater, which went poking his long nose about our boots, and made us look with some anxiety to our heels. From the balcony, which projected beyond the ruined city-wall in front, we looked upon the bay, and could see the steamer, which was to convey us, spouting smoke from its pipe, and wallowing, with its great black hull, in the swell of the sea like a huge whale.

Then there was a general move, and we passed down the great stone steps, through the ruined gate of the wall, out upon the yellow beach, and went straggling upon the long rocky reef, which stretches out into the bay, and exposes, at low tide, its black, rough surface for a mile or so. We toiled over this uneven path, which, with its jagged, sharp edges, its pools of sea-water, and its sloughs of mud, was particularly hard upon the French boots with which some of our party had honored the occasion. The curious among us, however, were compensated by an insight into the habits of the countless crabs which went crawling in and out of the labyrinths of the reef, which had been laboriously drilled through and through the hard rock, until it was as porous as a sponge, by the busy *torredo* worm. I lifted up, again and again, large masses of the hard stone, and could see round, white, glutinous creatures, strung through them, like candles drying in a tallow-chandler's shop. These worms are armed with a borer at the snout, sharper than any miner's tool, with which they cut out, and polish, through the hardest rock, a smooth passage for their bodies, which are as soft and yielding to the touch as boiled maccaroni. These are the worms so formidable to the shipping in the bay of Panama, and which destroy, in a few months, the stoutest hulls. Wherever there is a rent in the copper, or an exposed timber, they insert their borers without delay, and soon riddle a ship until she leaks like a sieve.

From the rough ledge of reef, we spring upon patient Negro backs, and are tumbled into the bottom of an unsteady whale boat, much to the inconvenience of white trowsers and linen jackets, and thence, with the hearty pulls and noisy shouts of the half-naked black oarsmen, transferred to the specie launch. This specie launch, in spite of a very uneasy motion suggestive of sea-sickness, and some very unexpected and awkward swayings of its long boom, which threatened perpetually first to knock the life out of a man, and then to throw his body overboard, we could not help having a very great reverence for. The richest freighted ships of Carthage and Tyre, the argosies of Ind, all the galleons of old loaded with the wealth of the Indies, of Mexico, and the Spanish Main, the opulent traders of London or New York, were poor in comparison with the wealth which had been heaped in that little boat, which, square-built, rough-timbered, and slouchy in movement, looked as miserable as any old miser, choked with gold and starved amidst his riches. She had carried in that dirty hold of hers near *three hundred millions of gold*, an amount not to be counted in a lifetime. I leave the miserable old hulk, with something of the disgust I should turn away from the scrooges who live or rather are dying daily, not far from New York, and who are no better than so many mud-scows, loading with millions, while they go on drifting through life without a thought of putting themselves in better trim for the voyage to eternity.

We reach the steamer *Columbus* two miles away in the bay, and, climbing up its black sides, are welcomed by the brisk Captain, cheerful and bright in his white linen suit, and are at once on our way to the beautiful island of Taboga. The ten miles' run in the bay was soon accomplished, while most of our party—

to which the various steamboat agents, with their wives and the Railroad officials, had added a dozen or so—were making merry in the cabin over the liberal supplies of wines and edibles from the storehouses of the Steamship Company, and a few lovers of the picturesque were watching, from the deck, the fine effects of the alternate rain and sunshine upon the surrounding hills of verdure, and the green Archipelago of islands, which were reflecting their varying hues and shapes in the clear waters of the bay as we sailed into the harbor of Taboga. The little town was lively with noisy acclamations on our arrival, and the steamers and shipping hoisted their flags, and reiterated charge after charge from their deck-guns.

Then was beheld the approach of the magnificent Captain Bob Swab, in imposing dignity, sitting in the stern of his immaculate gig-boat. The pennant waved over his Panama hat, and as he expanded that chest of his, swelling with the conscious dignity of a steamboat Captain, and displayed to full view those gilt buttons which glistened brightly on a broad expanse of white waistcoat, there was a feeling of wonder, not unmixed with awe, at the sight of so imposing a personage. "Who is it?"

was the question, passed in respectful whispers from one to one as the boat, after making a magnificent circle about our steamer, came up alongside, and out stepped a little fellow bringing with him an atmosphere which had a very distinct odor of tar, brandy, and tobacco, and making such an effort to look dignified, as he raised his little legs, that he started the eyeballs out of his head, and almost burst the gilt buttons from his waistcoat. It turned out to be Admiral Pomposity, better known as Captain Bob Swab, of the California steamboat floating yonder in the bay.

The *Columbus* put us ashore at the dock of the English Company, and when we had admired all the wonders of the ugly, black coal-houses and machine-shops, built upon the peninsula which juts out from the island of Taboga, and the beauty of the little cottages with green verandas which peep out of the trees, and hang from the sides of the hill like bird-cages, we were transferred to a boat, under the command of a mock midshipman, in gilt buttons and gold band, who finally—after having put back on several occasions, to give us an opportunity to wring our jackets, wet through and through with a succession of deluging showers, which washed out all our faith in the dry season—put us aboard the English steamer, where, while our party are enjoying the generous lunch of their liberal hosts, the reader may occupy himself with learning something about Taboga in the next chapter.

CHAPTER VI.

TABOGA. 1849 AND '50.

THE Island of Taboga is quite remote from the geography of most folks. But a few months ago it was quite out of the world—an unnoticed green spot in the wilderness of the Pacific. An occasional *Thunderer*, *Beagle*, or *Bull-dog*, of her Majesty's navy, would show its teeth there, startle the unbreeched natives, and leave a remembrancer in the shape of some runaway dog of a sailor, a seed of Anglo-Saxon civilization, which, well-moistened with grog, was sure to bring forth an abounding crop of drunkenness and riot. Taboga, in those days, was known to the English admiralty, and put down in their reports and charts as an island in the Gulf of Panama, with a safe harbor, good water, and an abundance of tropical fruit, pigs, and fowls. Yankee enterprise, while on the California trail, has at last nosed it out, and, without saying much about it, can show its fleet of a score or more of steamers and sailing-vessels, snugly moored in the blue water of

Taboga harbor. There is work there, and Yankee work, too. Large store-houses, built of Maine lumber by Yankee carpenters, crammed full of all kinds of marine stores, and sheds widely extended over countless tons of coal. Cincinnati pork in unnumbered barrels, and American provisions and ship-chandlery in endless variety. Large sea-steamers are leaving there weekly, with the regularity and precision of the Collins's line and the Cunarders from Canal Street and Jersey City. There are Aspinwall's fleet and Law's new steamers always on the go, starting and arriving, coaling and provisioning, in thirty days from San Francisco and back; and there are the English company's boats that, following in the wake of the Americans, have made Taboga their resting-place, and ply monthly between Taboga and Valparaiso, stopping coastwise at Callao, Payta, and Guayaquil, and other ports on the Spanish main. There is the taut little steamer, *Taboga*, no bigger than a fisherman's smack, that, to the wonder of all old sailors, spiritedly braved the terrors of Cape Horn, and now runs daily, from under the cocoa-nut trees of Taboga, to the very gate of the old town of Panama.

There is Aspinwall's agent building a bran-new house, of pine board and shingles, right among the wide-spreading mangos on the hill; and down below him, toward the golden beach, where before there was nothing but beauty, there is now his mournful-looking group of store-houses and bake-houses (with a biscuit-machine, an oven—fired with orange-tree wood and Welsh coal—and a brace of workmen, fresh from Yankeeland) all begrimed with pitch and coal tar, of undeniable utility and ugliness. Yankee agents and Yankee lumber, with a fig for the picturesque, carry the day hollow against palm-trees and orange-groves.

There is the little French *restaurateur*, Monsieur Jacques, in white apron and velvet capote, suggestive of *eau sucrée* and innocent dominoes, busy over the endless job of putting up and arranging his bijou of a café in that clump of cocoa-nut trees, which shuts him out from the yellow beach. Mons. Jacques is always in a fume; but in spite of his fuss and *mille tonnerres*, it will be months yet before the Café de Taboga rivals its predecessor in Mons. Jacques's good keeping at Bordeaux.

There is a party of expectant diggers, fresh from the States, encamped among the trees, awaiting the tardy arrival of some slow *Sarah Sands*, for which they have bought tickets in New York months before. They have spread their canvas tent, and made their India-rubber beds; they are sharpening their skill in cooking, and their appetites, over a pot of boiling yams; they are exercising their rifles upon the torpid pelicans or the rainbow-hued macaws; and, altogether, what with tropical skies, tropical verdure, tropical plenty, and a composing tropical atmosphere, they might be supposed to be leading a tolerably comfortable, easy kind of life; but they would give all they have, and all they *expect* to gather of gold in a week (no small sum), for a mere foothold upon that crowded steamer that is just off for San Francisco, with its throng of hundreds stifling with the crowd, the heat, and lust for gain.

Those drunken sailors—runaways—roaming about the beach, and quarreling with the natives, and those scattered, equivocal-looking people, neither one thing nor the other, made up from a confused medley of features, brought from Broadway, Dry Dock, down East, Kentucky, Wapping, Liverpool, and Hong-Kong; gusty-looking sea-captains, steamer-people, neither fish nor fowl; engineers, pursers, stewards, firemen, waiters, and expectant voyagers. These serve to complete a tolerably fair view of the island of Taboga, under the new dispensation.

Taboga has its traditions, in a small way; it is needless to go back to the days of plumed and painted warriors, glowing with cocoa-nut oil, red ochre, and savage glory, or to those times of the cruel conquest of old Spain, when she sent on the trackless path of discovery her bold bands, the dare-devil youth of Barcelona and Madrid, armed to the teeth, eager for gold and adventure. These were the ancient diggers, with sword in hand.

Conquest had settled down into quiet possession. Plumed and painted warriors were bearing the cross of the new religion, and had been saddened into patient hewers of wood and bearers of water. There were wealth and ease in Panama, cathedrals rich with golden and silver plate, monasteries abounding with treasure, sleek monks, meek of aspect, with overmuch of this world's wealth, when Morgan, the buccaneer, with a bold pirate's crew, was coming up the river, having taken by the way the high mounted castle at Chagres. He threatened to pounce upon monk and monastery, and to bear off the rich stores of silver and of gold. Taboga was near at hand, and there monk and friar hurried, laden with their much-loved wealth. The buccaneer, having laid Panama waste with fire and sword, was at their heels; and the frightened priests were fain, in order to save their lives, to disgorge their riches—precious heaps of tall candlesticks of purest silver, crosses and crucifixes, goblets and censers of virgin gold—very fair to look upon, and sore to part with. The old gossips of Taboga point with mysterious knowingness to buried spots of treasure. Some veteran cannon, yet reposing on the sunny side of a promontory of the island, attest an attempt at resistance, never carried out.

The Pacific Ocean rolls in a slow, heavy swell up the Gulf of Panama, for some ninety miles, until checked by the rocky strand that stretches out seaward for half a league from Panama—a warning to sailors, and a safeguard to the town—it is worked by the resisting rock into a fury of savage breakers, which go tumbling and roaring, and dashing against the high-walled fortifications of the town, and are thrown back in cataracts of spray. The ocean monarch meets and wooes his island beauties in a gentler mood; and here the course of true love does run smooth. He goes in and out among the fair groups, the verdant archipelagoes of the gulf, smiling upon them in smooth waters, gently whispering his love in a subdued murmur, and slyly kissing them with his moistened lips, in retired inlets and deeply-shaded bays. Taboga is one of a group of those islands which rise like pyramids of verdure, right out of the gulf of Panama, green with tropical growth from base to summit, from the blue sea below to the blue skies above.

On a clear noonday, looking from the high-walled fortifications of Panama, southward down a broad avenue of the gulf, formed by green islands on either side, the view closes upon Taboga, some three leagues away; its pyramidal summits look purple in the distance, and their outlines marked on the blue sky, show through the clear air as sharply traced as a drawing. The smart little steamer *Taboga* will whisk you away there within the hour; a ship's cutter, with four stout tarpaulin-Jacks, will pull you there in double that time; a bungo, with a fair wind and the ebb tide in its favor, may roll there in half a day; and a canoe, with a quartette of paddlers, in nature's sable suit, with much screeching, hard paddling, great expense of oil and sweat, and unlimited pulls at the aguardiente, will reach there somewhile in the course of time. When there, time, toil, and trouble are forgotten; the senses are first gently awakened, and then lulled by the pleasant influences of the island. All the tropical delights are there in overflowing abundance. The blue sky overhead, the clear blue water sobbing audibly upon the bosom of the golden beach, the rich growth of wide-spreading trees giving shade, the tropical fruit giving abundance, and sweet odors, and the moist, warm air soothing the body and nerves like a Turkish vapor-bath, all wrap you in a pleasing languor of body and soul. We are disposed to lie still upon its bosom; but let us look and stroll about.

The island of Taboga is about a mile and a half in length, and half a mile in breadth—about large enough for a good farm, or gentleman's country seat. Its length extends north and south, crescently inclosing a deep and secure harbor, sheltered from storm and wind by the promontories of the island, and the islet of Taboguilla, which lies a floating grove of green, facing the harbor. Taboga rises from the yellow beach, which frames it like a rim of gold, in several peaks, all overgrown with dark green wood and foliage, except here and there upon the slopes, a field of maize or yams. Strange enough, to the distant eye, these spots of culture appear the only spots of barrenness amidst the wealth of tropical nature. The ravine which divides the two loftiest of the island hills, is filled to overflowing with tropical growth, which seems to rush down in a torrent of foliage, that threatens to overwhelm with its green waves the bamboo village lying in its course at the base of the hills. The village, however, like some resisting rock, checks and divides the torrent, and it is borne on to the right and left in its flow of verdure, scattering here and there a green spray among the huts of bamboo. Down the valley, shut out from the sun by the shade of trees and entangled vines, with orange trees dropping blossoms in the water, a mountain stream flows cool and fragrant, finding its way past the very doors of the bamboo huts over the rocks, through the golden sand, into the blue sea.

There are, besides the main stream, two other smaller streams following a like course down neighboring valleys, and they all go on flowing night and day, cool and murmuring. These are perpetual fountains, shut out from the sun and hot day by an evergreen shade of tropical growth, ever ready to cool the parching heat and panting thirst of the endless summer of this torrid region. But the greater stream, which flows through the centre of the village, about which the natives have thronged like so many thirsty hounds after a hot pursuit, is the supreme fountain. This is the chief attraction of the island to foreign visitors. Saratoga and Cheltenham never drew to them a more gallant company than this trickling mountain stream of this far-off, unknown, little island of Taboga. Here, in these latter days of travel, fine old men of war, formal aristocrats, ponderous merchantmen, men of substance, hard-working and thriving mechanic steamers, master-workmen, fast-sailing clippers, fast-men and rakes, trim little cutters, pert dandies, come to take the waters. Here at the Taboga Spa they refresh, and drink in a new energy for a further voyage of life. They are not content with overflowing bumpers here, but like knowing men of the world they take in a goodly store for the future. About the stream may be always seen a jolly company of thirsty, big-bellied casks, tended by moist serving-men, drenched sailors; these big-bellied casks, old topers as they are, are not to be contented with a single pull, but go on, drink after drink, to their full, and are at last sent off reeling down the beach, and go bobbing and rolling unsteadily in the water, till they are towed alongside, hoisted in by main force, and finally stowed away in the hold of the ship, and tucked in with cleets and old spars. This will prove to be a stock of old Adam's best—the veritable Paradise brand—to be tapped, mayhap, on a stormy night off Cape Horn "when the winds do blow," or some thirsty day of a hot, stifling calm in the tropic; or in a hot pursuit after whale, off the far-away northwest coast; or homeward bound, within the sight of native earth and sky, to fill a bumper to those we love.

The natives of Taboga are like amphibious ducks, they are perpetually in and out of the water, they drink deeply of it, they bathe in it unceasingly, they absorb it at every pore, they are completely saturated with it. Many of the natives have, in consequence, a soft, limpid look, like a foreboding dropsy, and their children have great distended pot-bellies, and look, lying about naked, like pig-skins filled with Spanish wine, ripening in the sun.

Following the course of this main stream up the valley through the deep shade of a tropical forest, along a path worn by constant footsteps, and bordered by bright-hued flowers, scarlet and orange-colored, glistening out of full-leaved thickets of the deepest green, you come upon the Taboga bath. The bed of the stream is here widened into a natural basin of rock, bordered with flowering shrubs, and overshadowed with broad-leaved trees and a verdant net-work of vines and parasitic plants. A fall of water comes tumbling over some rocks hanging above, and striking with a gentle sound and a sparkling spray, fills the basin below, and the stream flows on its way. The traveled Sybarite may gloat over the luxurious remembrance of the completest of the *bains complets* at the Bains Chinois of the Parisian boulevard, of the magnetic and soothing influence of a Turkish bath, and yet he is but an anchorite in his imaginings, if he can not compass the delights of the Taboga bath. From a hot, steaming atmosphere, which dissolves the energy of the body, palsies the nerves, takes away all strength from the muscles, and loosens the joints, you go into the bath, and are at once "braced to man," muscles, nerves, body, and will, are all strengthened with a force before unknown, and fitted for yeoman's service. The change of temperature from the hot air to the cool water does not strike you with a chill and a shock, but you feel at once, with a sense of refreshing enjoyment, that you are in a medium most agreeable to the senses, and conformable to the comfort of the body. You can sport like a dolphin in this glorious bath, plunge into its depth, float upon its surface, or, with the rock for a pedestal, receive, like a water-god, the refreshing shower from the fountain above. This is the true Hydropathic establishment. Come hither, if you can, ye Bulwers, to cool your hot, seething, delirious brains!

From your bath you can see the native laborers passing to and from their work up the valley, where their rudely cultivated field-patches lie in the sun aslant the hills. Men, women, and children go trooping by, a crowd, of Egyptian hue, in scant, tropical costume —there they go—some carrying, poised on their swarthy shoulders, great palm-leaf baskets full of fruit, oranges, plantains, pine-apples, mangoes, yams, and maize; and others, women chiefly, bearing water-jars, monstrous in size, of a red earthen hue, and oriental shape and look. You can hear, too, the noisy glee of the women of Taboga washing in the stream, and catch a glance through the green trees of some coy maiden, a nut-brown Naiad, pouring from her calabash a cool and grateful shower, which goes unreservedly all over her beautiful person, that shrinks gracefully from the embrace. Strengthened with a bath, you are prepared for a walk; stopping in the village, which is on the way, for a draught of cocoa-nut milk or a calabash bumper of chicha,* poured out by the fairy hands of Dolores herself. Emerging from the village, where you have been dodging about the huts which are scattered irregularly about, and been stumbling over the rough rocky ground on which they stand, you enter upon the path which leads to the Tamarind Grove.

Tall cocoa-nut trees, nodding their green plumes high in the air, stretch in long array, fronting the sea, and guard, like so many feathered grenadiers, one side of the path which leads to the Tamarind Grove; while on the other side, up the hill, there crowds a vast mass of foliage. The redwood of great might and size, the spreading mango with its russet fruit, the orange tree with its glistening green leaf, its white perfumed blossom, and its golden fruit; the feathery-leaved plantain, with its heaped-up abundance; graceful vines weaved in every where, flowering shrubs, a thick undergrowth, the modest mimosa, the sensitive plant shrinking on the earth below, all intermingle in a confused abundance of green growth, luscious fruit, and brilliant color. The sun may be pouring down a hot blaze of light upon

* Chicha, a drink made of the fermented juice of the pineapple. It is sweet and slightly stimulating, like a mild beer.

the blue leaden surface of the still bay and its yellow beach as hard and smooth as a pavement of Sienna marble, but its hot rays are cooled by the deep shade in which you walk, and come in trembling on the path in a subdued and glimmering green light. The pathway soon opens into a freer space, where the tamarind trees extend over a level spot of earth that forms the southern end of the island. Inviting walks stretch winding in every direction through the trees, shaded above by the close intermingling of the green foliage, and lead as it may be to some palm-thatched hut nestling in the grove, or up the green hill into the tangled growth, or to the quiet bay, or down to the roaring sea-shore.

Happy, and careless as to time, we will linger and make a day of it in these ways of pleasantness and of peace. We stroll about with no object but enjoyment that comes unbidden: it comes in the warmth and softness of the atmosphere; it comes in the perfume of the air breathing the aroma of flowers and of mellow fruit; it comes in the bounty of nature that gives its rich stores with an open hand, making labor vain, and in taking away all doubt of the morrow, smoothes the wrinkles of care; it comes in the delight of the eye that looks every where upon the graceful forms of tree, plant, vine, and every growing thing, and upon the varied colors of leaf, flower, and fruit; and it comes in that sense of luxury that is felt by the glad guest of such a tropical feast spread by plenty and graced by beauty.

But we are human; we can not, like the chameleon, thrive on air; or, like the butterfly, fatten on perfume. We will therefore go in search of more substantial food, and take our way through the Tamarind Grove, down that by-path that closes upon a native hut hid among the trees. In the distance it looks not unlike some huge bird's nest half-covered with the leaves, and the languid native girl swaying in the hammock, and startled at our approach, suggests to the fancy the fluttering of feathers. It is in fact a native cane hut, and the hammock is swinging gently to the languid movement of a Taboga beauty. We enter, bending under the low open doorway, pushing aside the leaves, and doffing our Guayaquil sombrero and uttering our *buenos dias, Señorita,* with the most courtly air at our command. After a modest flutter and a graceful movement of light drapery that drops like a curtain over the full form and rounded limb that had been wooing the warm air in unsuspected secret dalliance, we are courteously made welcome. To our question, *Hay algunas cosas para comer?* we are answered a satisfactory *Si Señor*, and pointed to a corner where there is heaped up against the bamboo walls an abundance of plantains, bananas, mangoes, melons, *mame* apples, pines, and yellow oranges, fragrant with their mellow odors, and gushing with ripeness. As we look, feasting our eyes on the luscious heap, we see a monster of the alligator kind, a large, black, soft, fleshy thing, that seems to crawl torpidly about the heap: it has a long head like a serpent; its black skin hangs in loose folds about its throat, looking like the shrivelled neck ot an African hag; its body is thick and flaccid; the back is roughened with a bony ridge, and the belly, glistening with a slimy white, falls in folds about its spreading claws, and its viper tail coils in and out among the fruit. This we are told is an *iguano**, and an inno-

* The iguano is a favorite article of food on the Isthmus, and is served up generally in the form of a ragout. The eggs also are esteemed a great delicacy; they are of the size of those of a partridge, and are frequently removed from the iguano while alive. The writer has seen the natives rip up the animal's belly, which is as tough and apparently as insensible as leather, which it resembles in appearance, and having taken out the string of eggs, which sometimes amount

cent and much-prized item of the larder, and is urged upon us as a delicacy that an Apicius might smack his lips over. We shudder out a *muchas gracias*, implying a very decided no, to the offer of cooking this monster for our dinner.

Our hostess is a notable housekeeper, and while she is busy making ready our cheer, we have dropped into her grass hammock, into the very mould of her graceful form. As we swing in the hammock, we sweep the area of the whole hut, and examine the birdcage-like structure: its sides are made of canes placed upright and joined together at the top and bottom with cross-pieces, fastened by cords made of a native grass; the roof rises in a palm-leaf thatch that ascends in a central ridge and falls with a steep descent, bringing the eaves in a leafy fringe low down over the sides. The doors and windows, rudely cut out of the cane walls, open into the green grove. A great red earthen jar dripping with moisture, filled with delicious water, always kept cool by the evaporation through the porous clay of which it is made, standing in one corner with a goodly

to half a hundred, allow the iguano to live and run about, which it does apparently as well as before, until there is a demand for an iguano stew.

show of white calabashes arranged about, two or three hides stretched on the bare ground, some palm-leaf baskets lying near, and the swinging hammock fastened to the ridge pole, moving in its breezy sweep, are all the simple contents of the palm-thatched hut.

The goodly housewife, as we look about us, is in the mean time busying herself with the preparation of our feast, and although she labors with a notable zeal, all she does is done with grace of movement and a soft languid ease, that lighten all her labor. The plantains have been thrust into the orange-wood fire just outside the door in sight of the swinging hammock, and the dame, as she sits beneath the shade of a spreading tamarind, is busy dropping into a calabash of rice into which has been poured the milky juice, a shower of snow-white meat which she grates with a shell from the ripe cocoa-nut. The mealy plantain has burst its leathery jacket, and the rice mingled with the meat and milk of the cocoa-nut is done to a turn, and we feast; and our Taboga Hebe pours out for us a calabash bumper of chicha, in which her health and an eternity to her beauty are of course feelingly pledged.

For dessert we have no choice to make; we take what is offered from the stores of fruit, and are glutted with the sweets of the orange, the melon, and the luscious pine. To crown all, all hail our good friend, the wide world's friend, Tobacco! We ask for a cigar, and our maiden plies her ready hand. She has a store of the finest leaf Taboga grown, and culling the choicest from the heaped-up palm-leaf basket, sits at our feet rolling it into form. She spreads the broad moist leaves here, and there she heaps the drier fragments, and with her nimble fingers moulding the latter into shape, wraps them into the former with a cunning twirl; then she seals the envelopes with the exuding juice of the plantain, and lo, cigar after cigar rolls out before us in tempting abundance. She is proud of her skill, and throws back her unbound hair that had fallen like a thick black vail over her face as she bent to her work, and turns her dark eyes toward us in the hammock, and there is a smile of vanity in them, as she stretches out her hand grasped full of cigars, her cunning handiwork. We smoke and puff away the day in a lazy dream. We do not envy a Cuban Don.

The village of Taboga, with its hundred houses or so, and its white-walled church, we have described as lying at the opening of the green valley which divides the two loftiest of the hills of the island. From the bay in the distance, as we sail into the harbor, the little brown huts of cane and palm-leaf thatch look like the dwarf-houses of a Dutch toy village; and as they show themselves irregularly scattered about, peeping through the gaunt cocoanut trees that wave their feathery tops high above them in the air, they seem as if they might have been fixed in their straggling sites by the caprice of some child-architect at play. Some of the huts top the weatherworn rocks which divide the beach, and jut into the bay; here, upon the rocks, the pelicans may be seen full-paunched and torpid, dozing after a feast of fish with which they have glutted themselves in the waters below. Some of the huts are thrust back into the valley among the leaves that shade the stream which flows between the hills. Others, again, are grouped about the margin of the shore; when the tide is out, a wide surface of smooth beach stretches before them; when the tide is at its full, the waves murmur and beat at their doors. This beach is the chief approach to the island: here the boats land from the vessels in the harbor, bringing idle skippers to lounge about the village, bustling stewards to make their purchases of live stock, fruits, and vegetables, and busy sailors that go struggling up the beach with great water casks. The heavy ship's boat, with a strong pull of the oarsmen, is driven, lifted upon an advancing wave, high and dry upon the shore, while the native canoe, light and buoyant, with a gentle sweep of the paddle, seems to leap like a supple fish right out of water far beyond upon the sands. Here, upon the beach, the natives embark on their voyages to Panama and the neighboring isles, and here return. Here come from Quibo, the Islands of the King, the Pearl Islands, and other places in and about the gulf of Panama, large canoes heavily freighted with provisions, pigs, fowls, yams, and fruit of every kind, to supply the steamers and shipping. This beach, too, is the favorite resort of the natives when the cool of the evening breeze invites them to breathe the pure air; here the men lie idly about, smoking their Taboga cigars, and stretched among the fleet of canoes, left by the tide high and dry upon the shore; here the Taboga women lounge about, fanning themselves with the breeze, and cooling their bare feet upon the moist sand; and the naked children, with great glee and noise, sport with the waves, flying from the coming, and running after the going tide.

The native inhabitants of the village are a simple-minded, quiet, ease-loving, enjoying people. Existence, subdued and softened into languor by the warm, moist, vapor-like atmosphere of the tropical island, its drowsy repose in the still bay, and its fullness of sensuous enjoyment, and soothed with beauty, and fattened with abundance, seems like a long sleep. The various origin of the people shows itself in the occasional characteristic features of the Spaniard, African, and Indian; but mostly a general harmony of color and form prevails, giving the natives the look of the Egyptian race in their bronzed complexions, rounded limbs, and regularity of feature. The blood of the proud and cruel Castilian conqueror, the wild Indian, and patient Congo slave, mingled together, free of all harshness and bitterness, flows a mild mixture in the veins of the quiet Taboga people. They have all a sleek, well-fed look, and are unruffled and happy. The men are lithe and strong, and, though indolent, capable of labor. The women are full-formed and graceful, their movement easy and unrestrained, their features smooth and unvaried, and their eyes are large, full, and slumbering.

There is little need of work in this well-favored island. Food can be got by stretching out the hand to take it, for nature generously supplies an endless store; shelter and clothing are hardly needed, where summer lasts forever. The men, however, build cool huts of a native bamboo, and thatch them with the leaves of the palm, cultivate small fields of maize and yams, scoop out great trunks of trees, and launch their canoes upon the bay to fish, or sail to Panama, to barter their loads of fruit for the coarse cloth of Manchester, for their own use, and flaunting calicoes, cotton laces, bright-colored Chinese handkerchiefs, and cheap finery to adorn the women. The women keep at home mostly, swinging in their hammocks the live-long day, or busying themselves with their small household cares, tending their young, if mothers, preparing their simple feasts, or plaiting palm-leaf baskets, or pounding the maize, or otherwise doing the simple duties of their simple life.

As in all villages there are some notabilities who are thought to be somewhat better than their neighbors, and to have more claim upon the notice of the chronicler than others; so there are in the village of Taboga. First of all, there is the Padre, no reverend ecclesiastic of demure face and sombre mien, but a plump, jolly, "oily man of God," without a care or wrinkle, as round, smooth, and unctuous as a Spanish olive—no ascetic, who thinks that the joy of this world must be bartered away to secure the happiness of another; but a right merry fellow who never puts off to the morrow any pleasure that may be got to-day, and never giving a thought to the paradise above, seems quite contented with his paradise here below, and makes the most of his merry life among the orange-groves and dark-eyed girls of Taboga. He is a happy mortal, beloved of his simple flock, and an especial favorite of the Taboga women. By a free interpretation of the law of celibacy, or somehow or other, he has contrived to become the father of more than his share of the dark-faced and black-eyed urchins that indiscriminately toddle about the village. There is no better judge in the whole village of the fighting-qualities of a game-cock; and to see him to advantage, just look at him when he has doffed his canonicals, after saying mass in church on a Sunday, and observe how his smooth, oily face glistens, and how young and spry he looks, with his finely-woven Panama hat hung knowingly on one side of his black, crisp hair, and how gay, in his flowing white trowsers, and his bright, red silken sash, and how earnestly he thrusts himself among his cock-fighting parishioners, and bets upon the fight. He will outdance, too, any young gallant of Taboga at a fandango, and his presence always puts fresh spirit into the movements of the dancing girls, who think him the most lovable man in all Taboga. Though a cock-fighting and fandango-dancing parson, the Padre is not unmindful of his spiritual duties. Upon Sundays and saints' days he is always to be found at the church, surrounded with an odor of sanctity, chanting the mass with his oily voice, and he is always at hand to perform his spiritual functions at every birth, marriage, and death in the village. He has, however, a little *curé*—an infant Christ carved in wood, with golden hair, and red-painted cheeks—upon whom devolves much of the parochial duties on the more tedious of these occasions. At the earliest prospect of a birth or death, the little painted *curé*—who, by-the-by, is somewhat the worse for wear in the course of his heavy labors, and would be the better for a fresh coat of paint—is dispatched, to cheer by his blessed presence the suffering and dying, from his place at the high altar in the church, where he sits, cross-legged, at the spangled skirts of the wooden Virgin, in the worshipful company of painted saints and apostles. On saints' days, and especially upon the day of the patron saint of the island, Our Lady of Carmen, the Padre, all gilt and spangles, shows to great advantage, leading over the island, at the break of day, his procession of well-drilled vestals, all in white raiment, and with their dark, flowing hair decked with orange-blossoms, bearing crosses adorned with flowers, and carrying Our Lady of Carmen, gallanted by that glowing little Cherub, the little *curé*, under a canopy brilliant with gay blossoms, and odorous with rich perfume. We question whether the people of Taboga, the women especially, would exchange their favorite Padre for the Pope of Rome himself.

You may see, any day, at Taboga, a tall, gaunt, raw-boned, red-haired virago, her fiery hair streaming over her stringy neck and square, angular shoulders, and her bony limbs but half-covered with her scant robe, with a thin, wrinkled face, mottled with freckles, like a bit of parchment shriveled with age and spotted with mould, looking as fierce as the savage Bellona, and sitting as straight as a dragoon upon the back of a bull, that, with a slow, heavy tread, moves its great bulk about the village, guided by a meek Taboga man, old, deaf, and rheumatic. Jupiter and Europa! you exclaim;

the imperial and rampant Jove subdued into the tamest of bulls, and the enticing Europa sharpened into the sharpest and ugliest of shrews! The meek Taboga man, for one, we have reason to know, would not object to a celestial translation, if the taurine Jove should get up his spirits sufficiently to spirit away his Europa to the heights of Olympus. The red-haired Europa is Dona Juana, as she is called by the natives, with a due regard for her imposing dignity, the old Scotchwoman, as the irreverent strangers term her; the bull is her bull, the only steed kept upon the island, and the meek Taboga man is her servant-of-all-work and most obedient husband. Dona Juana is a thunder-gust in temper; and when she storms, as she often does, at her subdued bull and meek partner, her voice has the concentrated shrillness of a storm-blast, and pierces the air like an angry wind; all her milk of human kindness has long since soured—turned acid, doubtless, by the storms of her own conjuring. She is held in great awe, as she may well be, by all the quiet natives round about, and in great esteem, too, for her wondrous skill in physic. She looks like a sorceress, crouched in her low hut, the dirtiest in the village, surrounded with dirty bottles and filthy packets of drugs, mixing her medicine potions. What with her unsavory compounds of castor-oil, nauseous jalap, and the bitter stuff of her own composition, of which her nature would supply enough to store a doctor's shop, she makes, undoubtedly, a great impression upon her patients. How Dona Juana, whose rude Scotch tongue resists, like vinegar, the oily smoothness of the Spanish, and has an unmistakable smack of her native land, ever entered the paradise of Taboga, is a mystery. She is one of those stray waifs of humanity that, tossed about in the storm of life, finally drift to rest in the quiet places of the world.

The beauty of the village is Dolores, as soft, pulpy, and sweet as a Taboga orange. She is one of the full-formed beauties, ripened in the shade and repose of the island. Swinging all day in her hammock, and moving only in the early morning or cool evening, to take her bath in the Taboga stream, and living upon the nutritious maize and rice, and luscious fruit, she has become as white and smooth-skinned, and rounded and plump, as one of the Circassian women in the Turkish Sultan's seraglio. Her features have a dreamy, listless expression, though the fullness of her Spanish and voluptuous mouth, and the bright sparkle of her black eyes, save them from dullness and a want of interest. Her hair is a jet black, and flows in thick profusion over her rounded shoulders, which her low drapery exposes in all their glistening whiteness and full development. Her hands and feet are small and white, like those of most Spanish women, who take heed that no labor or exposure shall spoil their beauty, of which they are so proud. All fall in love with Dolores; but she is a sad coquette, and the world is warned accordingly.

There is Frank, the dark Maltese, a handsome Moorish-looking fellow, who has sailed and fought under every flag of Christendom, and done, it is whispered, dark deeds too, with slaver and pirate crew. He leads a jolly life; is a famous trader with the shipping, supplying it with provisions, and buying in return brandies, wines, and other stores, with which he supplies the sailors and natives from his shop near the shore. There is Slingman, too, a restless New Englander, who always looks like a shipwrecked sailor, who boasts of having been a lawyer in Vermont, a slaver on the coast of Africa, and American Consul at the Sandwich Islands. He has a Taboga wife, and is one of Frank's best customers for French brandy. But enough of these Taboga worthies.

The island of Taboga is free from all dangerous and venomous insects and animals; there are neither the scorpions nor the deadly vipers which infest the main-land, and some of the other islands in the gulf. There are, however, some curious, grotesque, and beautiful living creatures that surprise the eye of the stranger, and would interest the naturalist. There is the uncomely iguana, which is caught in the woods by the dogs, and much prized by the natives as food, for its rich and savory flavor. There are the land-crabs which burrow upon the summits of the hills, and once in a year come down in myriads to lay their eggs in the sands. The whole island is then alive with them on the move, the leaves and undergrowth rustle under their rapid, crackling tread; they come down in torrents, and their march through the island sounds like the pattering of great rain-drops. Then the natives feast; for the land crabs are choice food, and are to be caught on such occasions without an effort. They incontinently, in their hurried movement, rush down the hills into the huts, and go helter-skelter into the very *pot au feu.* On one day they are flowing down the hills in hosts, and on the next day they have disappeared like a shower. There are brilliantly enameled toads and lizards, whose bright colors of green, red, and yellow, glisten in the sun like precious stones. There is the macaw flaunting in the bright light with its many-colored plumage, and disturbing the quiet of the island with its noisy talk, and the gray-feathered, mild-toned dove, that hides itself in the wood. There is the busy insect, the *comyhen*, that destroys in a few months, riddling them like a sieve, the gallant ships whose stout timbers have withstood the storms of the ocean, and turns into dust the lofty houses of man's hands, the work of long and laborious days. There is the shrill cricket, that sounds from afar like the sharp blast of a steam-whistle, that the new-comers call the railroad cricket.

Among the full tropical growth of the island, its wealth of timber, leaves, fruit, and flowers, there is no limit to the display of the useful and beautiful. The *santo espiritu* blossoms on the island, in the dove-formed petals of which beautiful flower the religious sentiment of the Spanish Catholic devoutly worships a symbol of the Holy Spirit. Here too grows the *javoncilla*, a vegetable soap, the leaves of which, moistened with water, form a creamy lather, sweeter and smoother than the best Windsor. This is much used by the Taboga women in their baths, and to it they attribute their smooth skin and their rich growth of thick, flowing hair.

So much for the picturesque era of this beautiful island. Another era has commenced with California and the American steamers. Already in 1850, there were great heaps of coal stored beneath the palm-trees of the island, ungainly store-houses crowding out the orange-trees, great sea-steamers with their dark hulls, and vessels of all kinds floating in the quiet harbor. Bamboo huts turned into shops, with rum, gin, and other civilized commodities for sale, and filled with drunken sailors; the indolent native men, stimulated by gain, were hard at work, and the women had left their hammocks and had become washers of foul linen. There were strangers of all kinds coming from and going to California. The Bowery was on its travels, and it might here be seen in red flannel sleeves swaggering noisily about the quiet island of Taboga.

Taboga is virtually the port of Panama. All vessels make this island their resting-place. Panama, from its exposed and open roadstead, and the great rocky strand that stretches out for a league beyond the walls of the town does not afford a safe anchorage. Large vessels can not approach within three miles of the town. Taboga has all the advantages that Panama wants, a secure harbor, large and deep enough for vessels of the greatest draught, and a good holding ground for anchorage, an abundant supply of the purest water, and above all, a natural dry dock. There is a cove toward the southern end of the island, secure from all wind and storm, which stretches to a distance of three ship's lengths between two high banks of rock. When the tide is at the full, the largest ship can be hauled in afloat, till its bowsprit reaches the orange-trees at the furthest end of the cove closed by the island. When the tide, which falls almost thirty feet, is out, the ship will be left high and dry upon a smooth, hard beach of sand, gently sloping toward the bay, and the hull as readily got at for repairs as in any ship-yard. Some of the large California steamers have been beached in this cove, and extensive repairs made. The steamer *Oregon* was beached here and a portion of new keel put in, in a way which would have done credit to the ship-yards in the East River. There is, it is believed, no other place on the Pacific coast where similar repairs could have been done so well.

When the travel across the Isthmus of Darien shall have been perfected by the completion of the Panama Railroad, the little island of Taboga will be developed into the imposing position of a great Pacific port. It will be at the gate through which will pass the great caravan of trade, that will gather from China in the East, from Oregon, California, and Mexico, along the wide stretch of the northwestern coast, from the islands in the Pacific and from the far-distant continent of Australia, from the New Zealand isles, and from the long extent of the South American coast, from Chili and Peru.

Such was Taboga in 1849 and '50. Since, it and its inhabitants have undergone the usual vicissitudes of life. A fire, a year or two ago, destroyed a large portion of the native hamlet of bamboo-huts; and American civilization, being on the alert, planted at once a pine-board settlement, and now rows of shingle-roofed houses of Maine timber show their staring white fronts where once the palm-leafed cottages were grouped in picturesque irregularity among the tall cocoa-nut palms. The steamboat companies have built long docks, and added ugly store-house to store-house. Fleets of shipping still repose in the secure harbor, within the cast of a biscuit of the white beach; but the regularity of communication, which has succeeded to the helter-skelter emigration to California in 1849 and '50, has restored somewhat of its former tranquillity to the island. The California steamers have their dépôt there, and start every fortnight for San Francisco; the English steamers ply regularly from the island to and fro along the Pacific coasts of South America, and the little Taboga still repeats her daily visits to Panama. The loss of the picturesque is somewhat compensated by the comforts of the new civilization, and the traveler can console himself for the absence of the beautiful in the enjoyment of a cot with clean linen, and a good American dinner, inclusive even of homely pumpkin-pie, at the Pavilion Hotel.

But alas! Time has laid its rude hand upon some old friends. The little Padre, so juicy and ripe with life, while mellowing, a few years ago, in the sunny smiles of the beauties of Taboga, was suddenly struck down in an apoplectic fit, brought on by the fatigues of a fandango, in the course of a parochial visit to some of the dearly beloved of his flock, and now lies under a cocoa-nut tree, the leaves of which are heard to rustle moaningly in the silence between the beatings of the great ocean whose waves, in alternate tide, beat close by the Padre's grave. He died lamented by all the women of Taboga; and left a large circle of small children to mourn the premature loss of their spiritual Padre, and temporal, though unmarried, parent. Dolores, the beauty of the village, has gone the way of all flesh, such as hers. She has been swallowed up in the vortex of wickedness, and has left the paradise of Taboga for the less innocent region of Panama, where her character and her beauty are fast fading together. The hills of Taboga yet echo the shrill accents of Dona Juana, who resists decay like an Egyptian mummy. Frank, the Maltese, keeps up his supply of brandy, and blesses his stars that there is no Maine Liquor Law at Taboga; and, as for Slingman, he has gone to sea, to be wrecked the hundredth time, and thrown upon some distant shore, to resume his congenial occupation of beach combing.

CHAPTER VII.

RETURN TO PANAMA.

EXHILARATED with the day's enjoyment, and the flowing hospitality of their English hosts, our party reached Panama in a state of hilarious excitement, which, though more usual at the end than at the beginning of a feast, inspirited them to inaugurate the great banquet with immense vigor.

Monsieur Victor, the *chef*, had been busy with the full force of his vari-colored and polyglott household of French *garçons*, Spanish *muchachos*, and Jamaica nigger-boys, from early morning, and, having brushed up his fast decaying reminiscences of the French cuisine, had succeeded in extending from wall to wall, in the great saloon of the Aspinwall House, a brilliant spread. The true *artiste* revealed himself in a masterpiece of confectionery, where a locomotive of almonds was running down an embankment of sugar, ready to plunge into the depths of jelly below, while flags of the United States and New Granada, in candy, united their sweet embraces above. It was a triumphant success of high art; and the grinning Negro-boys, and the hotel-proprietor's greedy monkey, contemplated it with eager delight and watering mouths. The subordinate details showed the same high reach of ambitious art, and the whole feast proved the lofty imagination of the aspiring Victor, though the hungry guests would have gladly exchanged much of the esthetics of the tasteful Monsieur, for more substantial dietetics. All the grandees of Panama were there, beaming on the right and left, under the glowing hospitality of the impersonation of the great Railroad Company—the dignified Director, who headed our party. Bishops, Governors and Ex-Governors, Administradors and great Dons, a live American Minister, Consuls, Generals, and Vice-Consuls, hobnobbed in convivial conclave, and grew friendly and familiar under the social influence of a ceaseless succession of bottles of Champagne. Then the orators relieved themselves of the speeches which had long oppressed their memories, and the Spanish gentlemen, with true Castilian courtesy, submitted with a gracious patience to the oratorical English babble of which they could not understand a word, and took gentle revenge by inflicting in return some Castilian, equally unintelligible to most, but given in smaller quantity, and of better flavor. I need not say how eloquent all the orators were about the great event of the age—the union of the two oceans—the binding together the extreme ends of the world by iron ties—American enterprise, and other topics of glorification—and how Wall Street brokers and New York speculators were called benefactors of their race, in a way that would have brought blushes even to their brazen faces. The newspaper reporters were supplied in advance with all these effusions, and, of course, the world has read and admired their eloquence.

The banquet was prolonged far into Sunday, the noisy conviviality increasing as the wine was diminishing; and if the bishop had such a headache next morning as I had, I fear his ministrations at matins must have lost some of their usual unction. I knew I was more in a humor to curse than to bless on that holy day, and could have uttered a bull of excommunication against all wine-bibbing and dinner-spouting, with an emphatic vigor of denunciation to which the anathema of Ernulphus would have been as mild as new milk to burning brimstone.

The show of the Railroad Celebration was now over, and the performers prepared to depart. The puppets had gone through the required movements, had danced and squeaked before an admiring audience, under the cunning hands of the wire-pullers, and there being no further use for them, were, according to agreement, to be shipped to New York. So on Sunday, February 18, our party were once more on the railroad bound to Aspinwall, whence thirteen, out of the seventeen, were to sail for Havana the same day, *en route* to New York. Mr. B——, the agent of the Atlantic steamers, had, with his habitual generous hospitality, invited us to dine with his family at Aspinwall at five o'clock, and as the locomotive sped on at the usual rate of twelve miles an hour, and as the length of the road was forty-nine miles, and it was still morning when we started, it was not very unreasonable to indulge in the pleasing prospect of eating B——'s dinner that day. But all human things are uncertain, and the Panama Railroad particularly so. We had glided on smoothly for some fifteen miles of our way, had escaped the perils of the Summit, and the dubious chances of the trestle-work, and as the day advanced, lengthening the shadows of the forest, and the engine went puffing on, busily throwing its cinders into the eyes, our appetites gathered strength, and Mr. B——'s spread loomed larger and more distinct; but—c-r-u-s-h went something—"*Off the track,*" quietly suggested the chief engineer, who had been long enough on the road to be proof against any surprise; "*Off the track,*" dolefully echoed the company, as all hope of B——'s dinner disappeared in the certainty of passing the rest of the day and all the coming night in the wilderness. Obispo Station was not far off, so we tramped off in that direction; and finding a hovel there, with a sick Scotchman prostrate and alone in one compartment, and in the other a hanging cot, a rusty gun, two well-thumbed medical books, Cooper's Surgery, and Buchan's Domestic Medicine—a melancholy assortment of literature, which was somewhat relieved by a negro song-book—and a large collection of medicine-vials of all shapes and sizes, we prepared to make ourselves happy under such inducements to be jolly as Mark Tapley might have envied.

We succeeded in arousing two wild Jamaica Negro men from their lair, somewhere in the forest behind, and soon had a supply of salt junk and biscuit, and hot coffee, and a ragout, which the American embassador's wife pronounced exquisite; and which, out of compliment to the delicate sensibilities of that lady, went by the name of hashed duck, but which was in reality a delicious stew of young and tender monkey, as the black cook revealed to me, in confidence, after dinner. An abundant supply of Champagne had been brought along by our entertainers, in provident anticipation of an emergency, when vinous influence might be of assistance in keeping up the good-humor of the party, in case of a severe trial; and it proved most efficacious; for jollity reigned triumphant, in spite of the sick Scotchman, the medical literature, the monkey stew, and the night in the wilderness. How we warmed in admiration of the beauty of the tropical forest! how we gathered tufts of the sensitive plant and the golden flowers which grew at our feet, and gayly presented them in bouquets to the ladies! How we climbed the rocks, and brought back specimens of jasper and chalcedony! How some of us joked grimly over the discovery of a doctor's prescription-book, which I brought home as a *memento mori*, and have before me at this moment as I write, and in which I count something like 20,000 prescriptions for one month alone, and in which I read this melancholy entry:

"*John Watson and William Boyd to be al-*

lowed one day each for digging John Thompson's grave on Sunday, February 12, 1854."

John Watson and William Boyd must have had a grim holiday, bought at such a price, over the newly dug grave of John Thompson!

All hope of getting the engine upon the track in time, in spite of the tugging all night of hundreds of Negro-laborers, whose dark naked bodies, lighted up by the fires which blazed by the roadside, and loud shouts, likened them to so many demons, an express was sent off to Aspinwall, and a train arrived which carried us to our journey's end just at the break of day, and having breakfasted on the reserved dinner of the day before, the thirteen of our party went on board the *El Dorado*, and yielding themselves up to the safe keeping of that best of commanders, Captain Grey, sailed for Havana.

Four of us were now left: the Director kept busy studying, under the tutelage of the engineer at Aspinwall, the condition and statistics of the Railroad; Captain S—— went gallanting among the señoritas of Panama, to whose good graces he had commended himself by a residence in their midst some years before; M—— diligently pursued the ologies, gathering an endless museum of shells, rare plants, and animal eccentricities; while I returned to the cool comfort of the Aspinwall House at Panama, and had the run of its spacious halls all to myself, where I looked out the window for one half the week, and slept the other half. I condoled with the solitary landlord upon the desertness of his house, who had rewritten my name, with unusual extent of flourish, upon the blank pages of his book, and who despaired even of the steam-whistle of the Railroad awakening Panama from its sleep. My arrival brought tears of joy into the eyes of Negro Thomas, who brushed my shoes over and over again, in grateful acknowledgment of their companionship, and fancying a thousand times a day that some imaginary bell was ringing in his ears, his grinning face was ever peeping through my door with a civil request as to what I wanted.

I renewed my acquaintance with my opposite neighbor, who had not yet gathered up those loose robes of hers, and was still swaying in her hammock, swung within the balcony on the other side of the way. Her monkey threw itself listlessly over the balustrade. Her parrot was dumb, and the fighting-cock, which was tied by a leathern thong to her neighbor's door, drooped his feathers in the sultry heat, and ceased to crow. The streets hardly echoed a sound of life beyond the slow pattering of a solitary waterman's mule. The shops were deserted, and the Panama hats and blazing handkerchiefs hung limp at the doors, in the hot, breathless noon, without a passing bidder to notice them. Nothing could be more complete than the desertion and solitude of the old town; and the bells which now and then sounded from the ruined spires of the churches, seemed tolling the death-knell of the city.

Dissolved in the perpetual warm-bath of the hot, moist climate, oppressed with the universal apathy of the place, and feeling my energy oozing out from every pore, as the water was exuding, drop by drop, from that great dripstone at my window, I felt almost too indolent to move; and it was seldom that I could muster courage to go farther than Victor's, where I ate my daily meals.

I could think of nothing more refreshing one torrid, tropical day, than a visit to the Boston ice-house. Accordingly, arousing myself to the necessary effort, I strolled away to the Playa Prieta, hard by the railroad terminus, where I had read on a great wooden building, "Boston and Panama Ice Company." I was soon shaded from the hot sun within the cool recesses of the establishment, where the brisk agent of the Company welcomed me heartily, and refreshed me generously with a glass of iced water, with something in it, I dare not say what in these virtuous days of Maine Liquor Laws, which declare we are to have "no more ale," and will, by-and-by, deprive us of the "cakes" too. I was soon—thanks to my communicative Yankee friend!—well up in all the statistics of the business. I learned how a ship had left Boston with 705 tons of ice, doubled Cape Horn, and arrived in the Bay of Panama with a loss of only 100 tons, and how, in lightering this ashore, in the course of the long stretch of two miles from the anchorage to the land, the sun had reduced it to 225 tons: 400 tons of the ice, four times as much as had been lost in a voyage of six thousand miles, having melted away in the two miles of the journey in the bay. The speculation, I was sorry to hear, was not a very remunerative one, although the natives are getting over their dread of the ice, which they at first feared to touch as if it had been hot iron, and are gradually accustoming themselves to the luxury of sherry-cobblers and ice-cream, which latter is now cried nightly in the streets of Panama, in English, by Jamaica Negro women. Ten cents a pound—the present price—hardly pays the expense of bringing ice from Boston; and when the remnant of the stock upon which I trod, stored deep down beneath piles of saw-dust, and warmly tucked in with thick layers of charcoal, shall have been exhausted, as I was assured it would be on the 4th of July next, there will not be a lump of ice left to cool the hot thirst of all Panama. When the ice was first imported, it brought fifty cents a pound, and the Californian steamers were large purchasers at that price; but now these vessels supply themselves in San Francisco with ice at one cent a pound, brought from Sitka, in Russian America.

From the ice-house, a step or two across the hot beach, brings me to the Railroad Hospital, which, by one of those strange contrasts, ever occurring in daily life, is my next object of interest. Dr. R——, full of professional enthusiasm, welcomed me with a cheerful smile at the door of his lazar-house, black with decay, and rubbed his hands with intense satisfaction as he displayed to my view his "interesting cases." As I passed through the wards, with their floors dark with moisture, and their walls dripping with the exhalation of the neighboring swamp, and beheld the poor fellows prostrate on their low cots in the agonies of the malignant fever of the country, I could not but think that all the Doctor's acknowledged skill would be required to raise his patients from their beds, where they lay weltering in the very miasm which had first fermented their blood. "Ah! there is a beautiful case!" said the Doctor, throwing off the bloody sheet, and uncovering the mangled arm of a Negro lad. "A compound comminuted fracture of the arm," resumed my guide, as he deliberately took out his pocket-case of instruments, and selecting a probe, like an elongated ladies' silver bodkin, passed it in and out among a mass of swollen, raw flesh, bringing the blood at every touch, and contorting the face of the boy, until his great white teeth grinned like a death's-head. "I am in hopes," remarked my friend, "that I shall not be obliged to take that shoulder off;" a hopeful anticipation in which the patient seemed very much disposed to concur.

So we went in and out by the bedsides of the melancholy rows, the Doctor shaking his head ominous of death here, and rubbing his hands full of hope there. In one corner there was a Cooly, who, with his long limbs stretched beneath the white sheet in distinct outline, was as prostrate and motionless as a marble effigy upon a tomb; while his turbaned head and his bronzed Asiatic face lay still upon his pillow, and the only evidence of life was the hardly perceptible rising of the bed-covering above his chest, the dilating of his delicate nostrils, and the sad smile upon his thin lips. The Doctor shook his head, as he put his hand to the pulse, and dropped the arm, which fell like lead upon the bed.

Opposite, a brawny Irish laborer, with glaring eyes, a face glowing red like a furnace, his mouth gasping, his hot, steaming tongue protruding, and his great chest heaving, was tossing heavily about his bed, and throwing his great arms restlessly from one side to another. The Doctor rubbed his hands here, and whispered the remark, "Good constitution, excellent stamina, will get well." So we went from bedside to bedside, and room to room, until the Doctor finally led me out upon the piazza, where, in conscious pride, he displayed to me his collection of well-picked skeletons and bones, bleaching and drying in the hot sun. An anatomical collector would have watered his mouth over the gaunt show of grinning skulls and dangling skeletons of all races. I could not but concur with the Doctor's felicitations on his abundant opportunities for forming a museum, and fancied the poor Cooly's skeleton already gibbeted and rattling in the grim company of death's-heads and bony frames, which were so complacently exposed to my startled observation.

I was glad to be out again in the fresh air, which was blowing in from the Pacific, and rustling the cocoa-nut palms which shaded the hospital building. Extending my walk several miles further along the hard, yellow beach, I reach the ruins of old Panama, overhung with great trees, and covered with a thick shroud of tangled vines and undergrowth. Thus lie entombed the remains of the city founded by Balboa, three hundred years ago; the houses of which were built of cedar, very curious and magnificent, and richly adorned, especially with hangings and paintings. There were eight convents, two stately churches, and a hospital—the churches and convents richly adorned with altar-pieces and paintings, much gold and silver, and other precious things. There were two thousand houses of magnificent building, the greatest part inhabited by merchants vastly rich, and five thousand by those of less quality and tradesmen. There were the stables for the horses and mules that carried the plate of the King of Spain as well as private men toward the North Sea. The neighboring fields were full of fertile plantations and pleasant gardens, affording delicious prospects to the inhabitants all the year. The bold buccaneer and fiery Welshman, Sir Henry Morgan, laid all this magnificence in ruin, burning the monasteries and convents, the stately houses of the Genoese merchants, two hundred warehouses, and many slaves who had sought refuge there, hid among the "innumerable sacks of meal." The fire continued four weeks after it had begun. The pirates spared, in their cruelties, no sex or condition; and as to religious persons and priests, they granted them less quarter than any others. Not content with the captives in the city to exercise their cruelty upon, they scoured the country round for the fugitives who had escaped, and when they caught them brought them into the city and put them to the most exquisite tortures.

SIR HENRY MORGAN.

One poor wretch, relates an old chronicler, was found in the house of a person of quality, who had put on, amidst the confusion, a pair of taffeta breeches belonging to his master, with a little silver key hanging out; perceiving which, the pirates asked him for the cabinet to which the key belonged. His answer was, that he knew not what was become of it; but having found the taffeta breeches in his master's house, he had made bold to wear them. Not being able to get any other answer, they put him on the rack and disjointed his arms, then they twisted a cord about his forehead, which they wrung so hard "that his eyes appeared as big as eggs, and were ready to fall out." Not succeeding with these tortures in getting any more satisfactory answer from their victim, they hung him up by his private parts, giving him in the interval many blows and stripes. They then cut off his nose and ears, and singed his face with burning straw, "till he could not speak nor lament his misery any longer." At last, having lost all hope of confession, they mercifully ordered a Negro to run him through, which put an end to his life, and their inhuman tortures.

The old chronicler gives the history of a Spanish beauty who had fallen into the rough hands of Sir Henry, and whom that gallant cavalier entertained with lascivious discourse, trying to accomplish the desire of his lust, which the virtue of the lady denied him to the last. She was, however, agreeably disappointed in the manners of her wooer, for, says our historian, "this lady had formerly heard very strange reports concerning the pirates, as if they were not men, but, as they said, heretics, who did neither invoke the blessed Trinity, nor believe in Jesus Christ. But now she began to have better thoughts of them upon these civilities of Captain Morgan—*especially hearing him many times swear by God and Jesus Christ*, in whom she thought they did not believe. Nor did she think them so bad, or to have the shapes of beasts, as had been related. As to the name of robbers or thieves, commonly given them, she wondered not much at it, seeing among all nations of the universe there were wicked men, covetous to possess the goods of others." "Another silly woman, at the first sight of the buccaneers, cried out aloud, '*Jesus, bless me! these thieves are like us Spaniards.*'"*

Captain Morgan, having spent three weeks pleasantly diverting himself with burning churches and warehouses, robbing the Spaniards, and violating their wives and daughters, packed up his baggage, and took his departure with a train of a hundred and seventy-five beasts of burden laden with silver, gold, and other precious things, and six hundred prison-

* History of the Buccaneers of America. London, 1741.

ers, men, women, children, and slaves. On reaching the river, which passes through the delicious plain a league or so from Panama, the Captain put all his forces into good order, and, placing the captives in the centre, surrounded them on all sides with his men, and told his prisoners, in answer to their cries and lamentations, that "*he came not thither to hear lamentations and cries, but to seek money; therefore they ought to seek out that, wherever it was to be had, and bring it to him; otherwise he would assuredly transport them all to such places whither they cared not to go.*" "Many of the women," we read, "begged Captain Morgan, on their knees, with infinite sighs and tears, to let them return to Panama, there to live with their dear husbands and children, in their little huts of straw, which they would erect, seeing they had no houses till the rebuilding of the city."*

So complete was the ruin, and so terror-stricken the people, by the devastating cruelty of Morgan, that old Panama was abandoned forever, and the present city founded. A ruined tower, a remnant of crumbling wall, and a torn arch, almost hid in thick growth, are all that are left of the once rich and magnificent city.

* History of the Buccaneers.

The present city of Panama—the new city as it was then called—soon rivalled the old in splendor and importance. While Spain remained the mistress of the seas and her flag waved triumphant in the Pacific and Atlantic, the Isthmus was the great highway between her possessions in the East and West, and the city of Panama became the rich storehouse of her world-wide trade. There, were gathered the gold and silver from the mines of America, the rich stuffs, gorgeous products, and spices of the Indies, the enslaved Negroes of Africa, and the fabrics of Europe, brought by the richly-laden galleons of Spain, stored at Panama, bought and sold there, and thence consigned to the East and West. The traders of Panama were then the merchant princes who controlled the commerce of the world. The splendor of life of its inhabitants corresponded with their opulence. Palatial residences, capacious storehouses, imposing cathedrals, monasteries and convents, richly endowed with revenue and adorned with gold and silver plate and choice pictures, indicated the luxury, the wealth, and the ostentation of a prosperous people. With the decline and fall of Spain, and the loss of her dominion in the East Indies and the Spanish Main, came the ruin of the commerce of the city of Panama.

In the broken arches and crumbling towers of the city of to-day, its former magnificence is readily discerned.

The California emigration awakened the city momentarily from the lethargy into which it had settled since the loss of its trade consequent upon the declension of the power of Spain, and gave it life and activity, which were, however, but the results of a sudden spasmodic movement; and now, again, since the sounds of the California revolver are no longer heard in its streets, Panama hangs its head and slumbers. The American merchants and traders, who settled there, find their vocation gone, and are fast seeking some more busy place for their stirring enterprise. The regularity and rapidity of communication between the Atlantic and Pacific by means of the fleets of steamers and the Railroad, save the necessity of the diminished emigration to California resting by the way, and consequently give the inhabitants of Panama but little benefit from the transit.

The foreign inhabitants, who, in 1850, amounted to two thousand, have been reduced to a paltry hundred or so; and these are principally consular representatives of foreign nations, and officers of the railroad and various steamboat enterprises. The natives, amounting to about four thousand, are mostly of the common population met every where on the Isthmus—a mongrel race—in which the Indian, Negro, and white blood is indiscriminately mixed. There are a few families which boast themselves of pure Castilian blood; but I hardly think they could pass muster before the discerning eye of a shrewd Mississippi dealer in the Negro variety of mankind. The better class of inhabitants are government officials, ecclesiastics, and merchants; the inferior people are small tradesmen and laborers. Those who boast themselves of purer blood are unwholesome and effeminate-looking, evidently a race deteriorated by dissipation, indolence, and the effects of the climate. The mixed races exhibit some fine specimens of physical vigor, and the laborers show great strength and powers of endurance. The women are, for the most part, far from handsome, and, being ill-educated, have no social attractions, but are lifeless and uninteresting. The prettiest females are those in whom the Indian and European blood intermingle, producing that beautiful mixture of the *blonde* and the *brune*—where the former gives richness and the latter ripeness of beauty.

The amusements of the males are cock-fighting, fandango-dancing, smoking and drinking, in all of which the females occasionally indulge, with the addition of church-going, which is almost peculiar to themselves. They are all fond of cheap finery in dress. The men will give a month's wages for a red silk sash, and the women will sell all they have, and themselves into the bargain, to secure a tawdry calico. The better class of women are seen occasionally on the balconies, or walking to church, vailed in black, and have the conventional look of all the Spanish señoritas, who make you fancy there must be some Don Alonzo at hand with a guitar, a slouched sombrero, and a slashed doublet, ready at a moment's notice to scale a balcony, or do some other desperately-romantic piece of business. I had no means of judging of the intimate character of the Panamanian dames; but Lord C——, who had, spoke slightingly of their virtue, while he was rapturous on the subject of their beauty; but a young lord was a great temptation, and the ladies of his acquaintance must be estimated accordingly with a charitable consideration.

I got, one day, an insight into the domestic life of the foreign residents at Panama, by having called, very *mal à propos*, at the private residence of a bachelor acquaintance, with whom I had cultivated a counting-room intimacy. I surprised him at his chocolate, one morning, and having heard a frightened flutter—suspicious of the sudden flight of a petticoat—as I entered, I was not much puzzled to account for the fact of my friend taking his solitary breakfast with two cups, and could easily understand the loving proximity of a white waistcoat and a flowing robe of French silk, which hung in each other's embrace from the wall. I complimented my friend, as I swung coolly in his white, embroidered, Carthagenian hammock, upon the comforts of his bachelorhood. The odalisques, in scant drapery, smiled invitingly from the gilt frames; the guitar leaned idly against the wall, ready to murmur soft music at the gentlest touch; portfolios of French prints were scattered about the tables, and nude Cupids and Graces embraced lovingly before my very eyes. "Ah! you bachelors know how to take your comfort," I remarked; and as I spoke, I heard a subdued titter behind me, and, turning round in the hammock, and looking up, I could have sworn that the glitter of a pair of laughing black eyes flashed for a moment across the open space above the partition which divided the rooms. These partitions in the Panama houses never reach the ceiling, but are left open above, in order to secure a free ventilation in all the apartments, so necessary in a tropical climate. Female curiosity is thus spared the necessity of a keyhole.

I communicated my suspicions of a petticoat, and the possibility of a "little milliner" behind the screen, and bantered my Joseph Surface for his want of hospitality in not presenting me to the mistress of the household; when, not attempting to resist the invincible argument of the two chocolate cups, the female drapery, and the peeping eyes, he acknowledged that he did have some one to look after his shirt-buttons, and called out at once, in his soft Castilian, "*Venga mi cara Dolores!*" Dolores entered, all palpitating with timid surprise, half-curious, half-frightened. The red blood mounted her cheeks, and showed of a mellow ruddiness through her rich, olive complexion, while her face rippled, like a sunny stream, with a gleeful, childish laugh, and her parting lips displayed a row of teeth purer and whiter than all the pearls of the Pearl Islands. Most of the foreign residents form alliances of this kind while at Panama, and their *quasi* wives live as secluded as so many Circassian women in a Grand Turk's seraglio.

I joined, one day, the cavalcade of daily riders to the Loseria. After the heat of the day, at about five o'clock in the afternoon, the merchants, consuls, and other well-to-do residents, who have a horse or a mule of their own, or who can afford to pay three dollars for the hire of one belonging to some one else, clatter out of town on a ride, through the old gate, along the paved road, and out into the open country, which stretches a league or two from the walls of the city. The Loseria is a fine, undulating plain, spread with an ever-green covering of elastic sod, with a grove of orange trees in the centre, where the horsemen gather in rendezvous, smoke their cigars, and breathe their horses or try their speed upon the race-course marked out upon the neighboring ground. There is a glorious view from this spot of the Pacific, the gray old city, and of the hills of forest, and ravines of perpetual verdure, varying at every instant, in shade and color, as the perpetually-shifting clouds of the unsettled tropical sky rapidly vail and unvail the sun.

Among the horsemen gathered within the shade of the orange trees, was pointed out to me, as I rode up, the British Consul, a man of sixty, sitting his mule as straight as a dragoon, whose father was the celebrated Perry of the *London Morning Chronicle*. The son had, in early life, wasted on the turf, and at the gambling-table, the liberal fortune he had inherited from his father, and was forced to fall back upon the patronage of friends, who had provided him with the snug retreat of the British Consulate at Panama, which is said to bring him in the comfortable return of $20,000 per annum. With the Consul was a young English nobleman, Lord C——, who rode his horse, as all well-bred Englishmen do, with the firmness of seat of a Centaur. His thorough English, fresh-blooded look, with his cheeks mantling as red through his clear complexion as the petals of a rose, was quite refreshing in the midst of so many bilious-faced denizens of Panama. He rode his spirited nag, one of the best of the British Consul's stable, with wonderful address, and his lordship's white hat was seen in the distance, far ahead of his competitors, in the scrub-race on the course.

A group of us galloped away from the main party, across the plain, along a wooded by-path, up and down the hills, through the inclosure of a plantation of sugar-cane, to the door of a rancho, belonging to one of our companions, hung upon the acclivity of a wooded height, and buried in shade. After a short gossip with the dark beauty swinging in her hammock within, a cool draught of milk from a fresh cocoa-nut, and a parting cigar, we rode back to Panama, as night deepened the shades of the tropical forest through which the bridle-path winded, and the stars blazed out largely in the heavens, and the moon silvered the quivering leaves of the palm, and the fire-flies sparkled gayly, and the evening tropical breeze cooled the heated blood of our hard-ridden nags, and blew refreshingly in our faces.

CHAPTER VIII.

PEARL ISLANDS—CONCLUSION.

I WAS again at my daily post of observation on the balcony of the Aspinwall House, which had received an accession of life, in the shape of a half dozen travelers from Lima and Valparaiso, by the English steamer, on their way over the Isthmus to Aspinwall, and thence by the West Indies to Southampton. Two or three shrunk Englishmen in loose linen and slouchy hats, a tumbled woman with a bleached child nestling in the arms of its yellow nurse, a shriveled monkey, and a loquacious parrot, were welcomed joyfully by the desponding landlord, and they certainly enlivened the lone halls of his hotel—particularly the pale baby, the monkey, and the chattering parrot. Lord C—— had slipped through the eager hands of mine host, after having recorded his aristocratic name upon the books; and the proprietor of the Aspinwall House was inclined to indulge in some honest American patriotism against the British Consul, who had seduced away the young lord by the hospitable attractions of the Consulate.

I had exhausted Panama, and was tired of looking up the street, where the view seemed fixed within the outlines of the houses like a picture in a dingy frame with a prospect, made up of a bit of blue sky showing scantily above a roof and of a dash of green sea hemmed in between two white walls; with there a tint of yellow light coming from behind the swinging sign of the "American Hotel"—which hung before the hot sun, like a patch upon an inflamed eye—and with here the rising land with its vegetation clouded in a *chiaro oscuro* of smoke. Down the street was the same spire of the gray old church, with a bush growing out of its ruined belfry. Along the overhanging balconies were the same lounging women in loose drapery, the perpetual monkeys dangling from the balustrades, the fighting-cocks drooping in the sun, and the parrots hiding their heads under their green, stagnant wings. On the pavement still pattered the water-carrier's mule, and on the sidewalks the magnificent Padre displayed his golden buckles, the slouchy Negro women draggled along in bare feet, and the stout native porters shone in all their breadth of ebony back; the billiard-balls continued to clatter, and the indefatigable bar-keeper of the St. Charles did not cease to jingle his thirsty glasses. I was tired of this lazy monotony, and was glad when the promised expedition to the Pearl Islands was announced.

The stout Director, parboiled with the tropical heat, and very perceptibly shrunk in the boiling, had returned from Aspinwall, and was prepared to refresh himself, after his prodigious official labors in connection with the railroad, in the cool breezes of the Pacific. Accordingly, we were off, one fine day, in the steamer *Panama*, and sailed upon the broad bay of Panama for the Pearl Islands. In addition to our especial party of four, the remnant of the company from New York, there were the engineers of the railroad, some of the steamboat agents and their wives, a doctor or so from the steamers in the harbor, a grave Spanish Don or two, and the British Consul with his daughter, and the young lord in the white hat again.

Baskets of Champagne, with loads of luscious fruit and other stores, passed up the sides of the ship, and the great carcass of a whole bullock hoisted in by the sailors, who were singing as merrily, and pulling as heartily, as if they were intoxicated by imaginary draughts of the abundant Heidesick, and invigorated by choice fancy cuts of the best pieces out of the beef, in which their imaginations had full liberty to indulge, gave a satisfactory prospect of good cheer to us favored mortals of the cabin, which was realized in the substantial eating and drinking from the earliest to the latest sound of the ever-welcome gong during that famous voyage.

We floated along upon the tranquil waters of the bay, lounging in careless indolence, and satiating ourselves upon the choicest viands and the most generous wines by day, and wrapped in sweet sleep by night, while fanned by the gentle breezes which succeed, in the tropics, the setting of the sun. Hour followed hour almost unobserved in the uniform repose and calm enjoyment of the day. The sea was as smooth as an inland lake; the glare of the sun and the bright reflection of the azure heavens were breathed upon by a summer mist, and toned down in agreeable harmony with the eye and feeling. Green islands—paradises of verdure—succeeded each other in perpetual prospect. And so we floated on and on all day and night, until we saw the Pearl Islands glistening in brilliant green under the glow of the morning's sun.

Our steamer came to anchor in the harbor

of San Miguel, the principal town of the largest island of the group. The *Islas de las Perlas*, or *Islas del Rey*, are an extensive archipelago, with islands varying in size, from a green spot no bigger than the Bowling Green to those of several miles in extent. The town of San Miguel is situated at the northeast of the island of the same name, and is about ninety miles distant, in a southeasterly direction, from Panama. It is a straggling collection of bamboo and palm-thatched huts, and the inhabitants are of the usual mixed races of the Spanish, Indian, and Negro, where the latter darkly overshadows the others. Some canoes timidly approached the vessel as the anchor was dropped, and a few dark natives, in scant drapery, climbed aboard. The inhabitants of the town had been so much startled, as they told us, with the arrival of a steamer in their rarely-visited port, that they collected together their valuables, their pearls and money-bags, and hid themselves in the neighboring woods. One of the more knowing natives, whose experience had extended to the modern mystery of a steamboat, soon restored the people to confidence by assurances of safety, and the declaration that the United States was at peace with the Pearl Islands. With all their simplicity, they had a shrewd eye to their own interests, and were as eager as more civilized folks for a bargain. The men who boarded the steamer promptly turned out of their little cane-boxes, like pin-cases, the rolling pearls, which, passing from hand to hand, found much favor in the eyes of the ladies, and were finally purchased for a round sum by the young English lord.

The boats were soon lowered, and after a long stretch in the bay, we landed upon the reef, which extends out for half a mile or so from the white beach which borders the town. Straggling along this, some picking up stores of choice shells, some refreshing themselves with the green cocoa-nuts hurled down by nimble sailors from the tops of tall palms, which grow down to the water's edge, and others startling flocks of pelicans by their random pistol-shots, we make our way up the beach, through a fleet of stranded canoes, hollowed out of single trunks of huge trees, and go in and out among the huts of the town. Children of both sexes, and of all ages, from the toddling piccanniny to the supple youth, gather about us, and display their glossy ebony forms in natural ease and unconscious nakedness.

It was not the season for pearl-diving, but we were reminded of the *Islas de las Perlas* by the great square heaps of pearl-shells stored by the shore ready for shipment on the arrival of trading-vessels, the shells glistening in variegated reflection from the walls of the houses, in the dried clay of which they were inserted, with rude attempts at ornamental figures, and by the show of fine pearls of great price, such as might have bought the heart of a Fifth Avenue beauty, hanging in brilliant contrast from the shriveled necks of Negro hags, and flowing like rivulets of milk into oceans of molasses, over the flabby surface of their expansive black bosoms.

Of the fishery we could see nothing, although we had a couple of supple divers with us who had been expressly provided to show us the *modus operandi.* But that part of the programme was omitted as a concession to the ladies, I believe, and much to the disappointment of Lord C——, who had already made up his betting-book, and had given odds, barring the sharks, upon the wind of the little nigger.

Most of the inhabitants, men and women, seemed to have a supply of pearls, and, coming out of their doors as we passed, rolled out upon their black palms streams of the brilliant products of the island. One coal-black fellow—the Rothschild of the place—showed us a collection of his valuables which amounted, in the aggregate, to $100,000, and among which there were pearls as large as a boy's marble. Some of our companions, thoughtful of a sister or a sweetheart at home, made some purchases, probably not to the disadvantage of the sellers. The day speedily passed away, with roaming about the straggling town, inspecting its treasures, haggling with the pearl-traders, admiring the ebony maids, and exercising the stranger's privilege in staring at every thing, and every body.

The steamer, having weighed anchor in the evening, reached Taboga at an early hour next morning, where I spent a day or so in the enjoyment of the delights of the natural beauties of that paradise of islands, and in the comforts of the civilized appliances, cleverly administered by the cunning hand of mine host of the Pavilion Hotel, and then re-embarked on board the little steamer *Taboga*, and was landed in an hour at the gate of the crumbling walls of Panama.

I had hardly taken possession of my expansive quarters at the Aspinwall House, when the Jamaica boy, Thomas, came grinning in with the intelligence that the California steamer had arrived; and on looking down the street a moment after from my balcony, I saw a straggling crowd of characteristic red shirts, slouchy hats, and blankets making their way into the town under the guidance of a hotel-scout, who was, with commendable enterprise, leading the flock to the American Hotel—"the best house in all Panama." It was now time to bid farewell to the old city, and speed on my way homeward.

On arriving at the Railroad Station, I pushed through a noisy throng of Californians, struggling in confused contention, and sweating in the hot sun under their loads of baggage, at the ticket-office, and denouncing, with great vigor of language, the charges of the Railroad Company. One tall fellow, with the growth of beard of a Turk, and with an ugly face, roughened with the wild experience of a miner's life on the Sacramento, brandishing his red shirt-sleeves, was immensely emphatic, and shouted, "Come out with your sacks in your hand, I'll see you through." In spite, however, of this bluster, the crowd soon settled into quiet groups, and cooled their hot impatience to be on the move with draughts of iced-water, ginger-beer, or the refreshing fruits which the Jamaica Negresses and the natives were, with clamorous eagerness, pressing upon the throng.

From the door of the Station, I looked out upon the bay. Four large steamers blotted out, in great black masses, the otherwise brilliant surface of the water, sparkling in the midday sun. There was the *Golden Age*, just arrived from San Francisco, the *John L. Stephens*, awaiting the New York passengers for California, the English steamer *Bolivia*, bound to the South American coast, and the British steamer, the *Virago*, gloriously distinguished as a peaceful messenger of hope and mercy to Strain and his party, the relation of whose heroic endurance in *Harper's* we can hardly read for the tears in our eyes, and less gloriously notable as a man-of-war in the bloody struggle at Petropaulowski. The *Virago* had just unshipped a cargo of a million and a half of treasure, brought from the coast of Mexico, which, in spite of the railroad, has, as in the olden time as far back as the days of the Spanish galleons, been conveyed across the Isthmus on the backs of mules.*

The specie launch has grounded upon the white shore, just below me, and stout Negroes go splashing in the water to the boat's side, and heaving upon their naked, black shoulders

* The gold and silver brought by the English men-of-war from the Mexican coast, and by the steamers from the South Pacific, are not conveyed across the Isthmus by railroad, in consequence of the charge of one half per cent., being double the expense by mules.

the iron-bound boxes—each one a fortune, packed with gold dust, valuable ingots, and golden coin—return toiling up the beach, and deposit their loads, rattling with the clink of the precious metals, into the treasure-car of the train. The ragged guard, armed with their rusty firelocks, are ranged in straggling squads about the gold-bearers with a show of protecting power which should be very encouraging to the anxious eyes of Wall Street. Within reach of me, bound fast to the leaning trunk of the cocoa-nut tree which shades the door where I stand, there is a sullen Negro desperado, who has been caught in the act of placing a stone upon the railroad track, with the acknowledged intention of hurling some hundreds of mortals into eternity, by the way of one of the steep ravines which open their jaws fearfully in the course of the road. With more faith in the strong cords which tighten around the wrists and ankles of the black villain until his dark veins swell like coiling serpents, than in those rusty firelocks in the undisciplined hands of the ragged guard, I can calmly behold the vengeance threatening in his glistening white teeth and scowling face.

The steam-whistle pierces, with its shrill echo, through and through the trees; there is a helter-skelter rush of red shirts up the bank and into the cars; a shout of "El ferro-carril!" from the noisy crowd of natives, and we plunge into the forest on our way to Aspinwall. In the corner opposite to me is the young lord in the white hat again, vainly trying to abstract himself with a book from the noisy throng of smoking, chewing, and salivating, half-dressed democrats who throng the car.

In four hours and a half from the last view of the Pacific, we were again upon the shores of the Atlantic ocean; and as the expected steamer from New York had not arrived, the passengers yielded themselves up, with growling impatience, to a night's breath of the poisoned atmosphere of Aspinwall.

I found the usual warm welcome from the Railroad officials at the "Mess House," and familiarly entered into possession of my old quarters, when the little, bustling steward came in, with a long and portentous expression of face, and informed me that my room had been appropriated to a young English lord, and that he would conduct me to another apartment, where, at any rate, there would be no want of company, as I should find two other occupants beside myself. I, of course, deferred at once to the "young English lord," as I was bound to do, being his elder by a dozen years or more, and only a republican.

Lord C—— was accordingly installed, as he was justly entitled, doubtless, in my room; and, in accordance with hereditary right, placed in the highest seat at the dinner-table. It was edifying to behold him when he rose so reverentially to the grace after meat of the chaplain, and particularly when, as he lit his cigar a minute afterward, his lordship so emphatically denounced that reverend personage as a "damned Methodist."

Under the social influences of the "Mess House," as we gathered on the piazza to cool ourselves in the sea-breeze blowing fresh over the Atlantic from our northern homes, and to beguile our anxious impatience for the arrival of the steamer, the young English lord became very communicative. It was as good as reading a shilling novel to listen to his history, with a romantic episode in it, which would have supplied Thackeray with a piquant chapter for his "Newcomes," and Mrs. Gore with material for three volumes at least. The young sprig of nobility informed us how he, an offshoot from the noblest stock of the old Norman aristocracy, the eldest son of an English earl, and heir-presumptive to an English duke, with all the blood of all the Howards enriching his veins, had fallen in love with his sister's governess; and his lordship seemed to think, like the Marquis of Farintosh, in the April number of the "Newcomes," "even if she were a beggar-girl, that, if he elevated her to his sublime rank, the inferior world was bound to worship her."

The paternal Earl, however, and the maternal Countess, were not so ready to mix their patrician ichor with the blood, however wholesome, of a miserable governess. Accordingly the young heir, after a more than usually intense love passage with his lady-love, was sent back to his tutor at Cambridge, where, still resolute in his determination to persevere in his courtship with the governess, as was daily made manifest through the post-office, in spite of the distraction of academic breakfasts and college studies, it was resolved by the noble head of the noble house, that his youthful scion should be transported beyond seas. So the young lord was shipped to Australia, where, after a year's absence, his anxious parent wrote him a paternal epistle, in which he expressed the hope that all "that nonsense about the governess had been forgotten." To which the son replied with a constancy worthy of a Leander, that the wide sea was no barrier between him and his love; and took the occasion of the same post to propose in form to the guardian of his sweetheart, some merchant, Brown, Smith, or Jones of Liverpool, for her hand.

In the course of months, while his lordship was being roughly elbowed among the rude democracy, and his aristocratic sensitiveness tempered in the hard experiences of Australian life, another paternal epistle arrived, in which the proud Earl frankly acknowledged the pluck of his boy, and gave a reluctant consent to his marriage with the governess, who turned out to be not so lowly-born after all, her father having been a Colonel in the British army, with some faint spice of aristocratic descent embalming his memory. The young lord, rejoicing in his triumphant love, took ship at once for the coast of Peru, and thence to Panama and Aspinwall, hastening to the embraces of the governess, who, if the *London Times* will leave the lords and ladies alone, has a good chance of wearing a ducal coronet, and undergoing a matamorphosis which will make Cinderella a tame heroine in comparison.

"Look, there is the steamer! hurrah!" and there indeed she was, making right for us, plunging her black nose into the rising swell, rolling her hull, spouting her smoke, which gathered to the horizon in great clouds, and coming rapidly every moment into more distinct view. It is the *Illinois*, and we are at once in the bustle of preparation for departure. In a few hours the steamer has emptied out her miscellaneous crowd of passengers into the railroad cars, and having taken in an equally miscellaneous throng, turns round and steams back to New York.

Lord C—— and I were paired in a stateroom on deck, which I, with a vivid recollection of the shelves on board the *George Law*, thought luxurious, but his lordship grumbled at as rather constrictive of his lordly importance. Dick, the Negro steward, was in raptures on the discovery of a living lord within the scope of his administration, and from that moment commenced a series of faithful attentions, which, though concentrated upon my aristocratic companion, did not fail to benefit me by their reflected lustre. I would recall here, with grateful remembrance, Dick's untiring devotion, by night and by day, manifested in unlimited broiled bones, anchovy toasts, and iced punches, abstracted by his cunning hand from the vigilance of the head steward when the Argus eyes of that functionary were closed in sleep, and the key of the pantry was in his pocket, long after the ship's bell had struck midnight, and in the appetizing breakfasts hot from the galley, ingeniously conveyed at most unseasonable hours to No. 10; when No. 10 was cleverly put down by Dick on the sick list, though evidently, whatever may have been the other symptoms of that afflicted compartment, loss of appetite was not the most prominent. Dick, I fear, was sadly debauched by his too intimate association with aristocracy, and so rapidly assimilated by his easy compliance, that he came at once within the category embraced by the old proverb, "Like master, like valet."

These sea-voyages are all alike, so I need not say how we ate and drank all day and slept all night, with occasionally reversing the process, and doing considerable diurnal sleeping and nocturnal drinking, for variety's sake. Day followed day in lazy succession, as the ship floated smoothly over the calm seas, and with the gentle breezes of the tropics. As the soft air of the perpetual summer breathed upon us, we sunk, "with joints unknit," into a slumbering indolence, and were almost without a consciousness of existence, until the ship sailed into the troubled seas of northern latitudes, and, breasting northern gales, trembled to her lowest timbers with the shock, and sent us all, shivering, out of our linen jackets into our overcoats.

The Captain, than whom no better sailor commands a ship, and in the employment of whose skill and resolute energies, in the approaching expedition to the Arctic Ocean, the Government has secured the strongest hope for the safety of the adventurous Kane, was determined to relieve the monotony of the voyage, and got up a scene for our amusement. He directed his course straight for Cape Antonio at the western extremity of Cuba, and fluttered the Spanish fleet dozing there, one night, and startled them with a terrible nightmare of an impending fillibuster. The Dons awoke, and while they were rubbing their eyes, the steamer moved rapidly on by the fleet, and was far out of the range of gun-shot when the Spaniards began to blaze away in the dark, making a very pretty display of fire-works from the black hulls of their ships, suddenly lighted up as brightly as daylight, which compliment our Captain returned with a show of rockets and blue-lights from the fast-departing poop of his saucy ship.

There is all the difference between going and returning Californians that there is between hope and disappointment, and it was observed that our sea-companions on the homeward voyage were infinitely less hilarious than those who were outward-bound. They were bringing little property home with them beyond their blankets and red shirts, and these were sadly the worse for wear. Some one or two of the cabin-passengers boasted of fortunes, but this was before the tornado of bankruptcy had swept away the golden harvest of California. There was one, a Californian coach proprietor, who was put down as worth his million or so, although it was not a half dozen years since he had held the reins himself as a driver of a coach in the State of New York, and who had the usual astounding Californian incidents to relate which will not be believed a score of years hence. He had paid, he said, one hundred gold ounces (sixteen hundred dollars), for shoeing twenty-five horses in Sacramento, and had given his hostler two hundred dollars a month —an income the governor of a State might envy —and moreover, he avowed that the present occupant of that responsible position was no less a personage than a retired banker, who had made quite a figure in the financial world, until his credit unfortunately gave out, and he was obliged to seek retirement in bankruptcy.

There was a storm in the course of the voyage to be sure, as no voyage is complete without a storm, and the sailors said it blew dogs and cats, and that they had never known it blow harder, and that the *Illinois* was the finest boat in a sea they had ever sailed in. It did blow indeed, and the ship tossed, and the beams cracked as if they were about snapping in two, and the soup-tureen upset, and the roast pig gave a lurch to port, and down it went into the lap of our Director's best pair of trowsers. There was no sleep in our berth on deck that night, not that his lordship and I were frightened, but we were uncommonly sociable, and it was so pleasant to hear human voices in the midst of the awful roar and tumult of the wind and the sea. There was no damage done beyond the wreck of his lordship's white hat, which, having gallantly buffeted all night with the waves, which washed to and fro in our cabin, knee deep, finally drifted into the —— in the morning.

The storm, however, gave us an opportunity of extending our traveling experiences to Norfolk, where the steamer put in for coal, having consumed so much fuel in struggling with the gale. We accordingly sailed through Hampton bay, passed old Point Comfort, the Rip Raps, the mouth of James River (Jeames they call it), came to anchor in the harbor, facing the mouth of the Elizabeth River, with the great hull of the leviathan ship the *Pennsylvania* walling up the view, and I landed in the city on a solemn Sunday, walked up a solemn street with a defunct hotel at one end of it, ate some oysters which were excellent, drank some apple toddy which was execrable, and, resisting the attempt of the landlord of the sole surviving hotel to put me to bed in company with two strangers, notwithstanding the assurance that they were gentlemen of the first standing, I returned at night to the ship. Next day the *Illinois* sailed for New York, and in thirty hours reached the dock at the foot of Warren Street, where I jumped ashore and landed, knee deep in the snow, upon the same spot I had left just five weeks before.

I had, before leaving the ship, shaken a farewell hand with Lord C——, who, on parting, had courteously remarked that he would be happy to see me, if ever I should visit England, at C——, one of the most stately ducal palaces in all England—which I told him I had already visited, having been hospitably conducted through its noble halls by a polite though loquacious housekeeper, for the small consideration of ten shillings sterling. "Ah!

then you probably recollect my portrait, which hangs in the grand picture-gallery next to Landseer's Bolton Abbey?" was his remark. I did recollect the Bolton Abbey—for who can forget such a picture?—but I was obliged to confess my ignorance of the counterfeit presentment of the handsome young fellow who then stood before me, who, I could not but think, would make a very good portrait for a Court-artist, with his lithe figure, his high-bred face, his thin lips with their slight, supercilious curve, expressing a resolute determination to have his own way, and a contemptuous disregard of any other way but his own, his full, curved chin, his delicately-chiseled nose, and clear, arched forehead crowned with dark-brown hair closely matted in a luxuriance of curls. I bid his lordship good-by; and my last sight of the summit of his white hat was through a forest of whips of surrounding hackmen. I have been thus particular in regard to my last interview with Lord ——, as there is a mystery not yet cleared up in regard to him, which gives interest to his person, which, however dearly we may love a lord, it might not otherwise possess.

M——, of our party, had been invited very pressingly to dine with Lord C——, the day after our arrival, at the St. Nicholas Hotel, where his lordship, as he said, had determined to install himself. M—— accordingly proceeded to the hotel at the time appointed (seven o'clock, I believe, was the aristocratic hour), and to his peremptory demand, made in the certainty of a dinner under the most promising auspices, to be shown to the room of Lord C——, he was told by the bar-keeper, with the coolest indifference, that no such gentleman was, or had been, in the place. From the St. Nicholas, M—— went to every hotel in the city, cross-questioning all the bar-keepers, and sifting all the books, but heard of no Lord C——. The British Consulate was next tested—still no traces of Lord C——. The Cunard steamer agency's passenger-lists were then investigated, with no better result. The police were put on the scent, but in vain. The telegraph gave no satisfactory answer to the questions which flew along its wires.

Nothing has yet been heard of Lord C——. Whether his lordship was in such a hurry to rush to the embraces of the governess and future duchess, that he could not stop to dine at New York, or whether he found it convenient to assume an *incognito* for concealment, in order to avoid the inconvenience of the settlement of a *poker* account, I do not know; but that his lordship did leave a *poker* account unsettled, I do know. He, early in the voyage, became dissatisfied with the slowness of two-shilling whist, and, confident in his skill at *poker*, which he confessed to having acquired from some shrewd Yankees at the cost of a thousand pounds, he devoted himself to that tempting game, by which he became a debtor, in the books of some astute Californians, to the amount of several hundreds of dollars. This debt was left unpaid, not from any want of means, for I saw an abundance of money in his possession; and surely not from dishonesty, for it is preposterous to suspect that a lord *in esse*, and a duke *in futuro*, would fly from a debt like a runaway rogue.

There is but one other supposition left, which would leave the fame of his lordship untarnished, but deprive the peerage of Great Britain of a promising scion, and the poor governess of a coronet; it is, that some prowling thieves and assassins had laid hold of him, in the confusion of the crowd and in the darkness of the night, on the arrival of the steamer, and, with a hand on his throat, had throttled and then rifled him of the signet-ring he wore, his watch, and his purse, and thrown his body from the dock into the North River. That he was veritably Lord C——, we had the word of the British Consul at Panama, who ought to know, and who entertained him at his house; that he gave intrinsic evidence of what he pretended to be, none of his companions doubted for a moment.

THE END.

www.ingramcontent.com/pod-product-compliance
Lightning Source LLC
LaVergne TN
LVHW050519100826
845148LV00002B/384

9781425521455